Homemade
Christmas

Homemade
Christmas

Create your own gifts, cards,
decorations, and recipes

Contents

Homemade Gifts

Homemade Edible Treats

Introduction

For many people, Christmas is their favourite time of year: decorating the home and tree, wrapping and sending presents, and bringing together friends and family. This year, create a truly unique and crafty Christmas by making your own festive decorations, unique gifts, and delicious Christmas desserts and snacks.

Every idea in *Homemade Christmas* is explained in step-by-step detail so you can achieve delightful, professional-looking results. There are lots of ideas for how you can add your own twist, so you can make this Christmas perfectly yours.

Get into the Christmas spirit and begin!

Homemade Decorations

Dried leaf wreath

Dressing your front door with a wreath at Christmas time helps to create a wonderfully warm, festive welcome to your home. The only downside is that you can't enjoy the wreath indoors. The solution is to hang another, more delicate, decorative wreath in your living room or hallway: collect fallen leaves and seed heads in the autumn and turn them into this stunning arrangement.

Materials

- Richly coloured leaves
- Sheets of newspaper
- 1 large wire wreath frame, available from florists or online retailers
- Thin wire
- Mesh ribbon
- Staples
- Eco-friendly adhesive glue

Tip

Collecting leaves

Look for fallen leaves in early and mid-autumn before the weather takes its toll. Red oak (*Quercus rubra*) and maple (*Acer*) are good choices. Depending on the room temperature and type of leaf, they can take up to a week to dry out and flatten.

1 Arrange leaves in a single layer between sheets of newspaper under a mat or piece of carpet, or place a couple of heavy books on top.

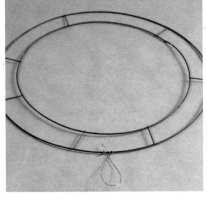

2 Once the flattened leaves are completely dry, make up the wreath. Secure the wire in a loop and attach it to the top of the frame.

3 Wrap the mesh ribbon around the frame in a zig-zag fashion. Staple it onto the frame at intervals to cover the frame completely.

4 Glue large leaves onto the mesh, stems pointing inwards, so that they overlap slightly. Glue small leaves on top in an even pattern. Allow to dry.

Fabric garland

This charming garland is versatile enough to decorate mantlepieces, kitchen dressers, Christmas trees, and bedrooms. Store it carefully and it can be reused every year. You can even make your own felt by washing an old, cream-coloured 100 per cent wool blanket or garment on a hot machine wash.

Materials

- Garland templates (pp.232–35)
- Large piece of cream-coloured felt
- Brown felt for the gingerbread men
- Scissors
- Pins
- Eco-friendly fabric pen
- Coloured embroidery thread (for blanket stitching and features) and needle
- Ricrac trimming
- 5 lengths of wire, each about 8cm (3in) long
- 1m (3ft) twine or string
- Pieces of recycled ribbon
- Old woollen garment or scarf
- Recycled buttons

1 Cut and pin together two of each shape from cream felt, and two gingerbread men from brown felt. Decorate one stocking with the pen.

2 Sew the shapes together. Leave the mitten and stocking tops unsewn. Sew on the features and ricrac trimming (see pp.18–19).

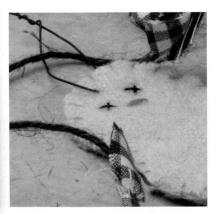

3 Thread a piece of wire through the top of each shape and secure in a loop. Thread the twine through the loops and tie ribbons onto the twine.

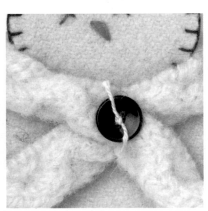

4 Cut strips from the garment for scarves and sew them, together with some decorative ribbons and buttons, onto the fabric shapes.

Mitten Sew a folded length of recycled ribbon and a vintage button onto the front of the mitten. Leave the top unstitched.

Robin Cut a circle of fabric (p.235), fold in half, insert a fabric beak, and sew the curved edges together. Add wings and a red breast.

Christmas tree Cut two tree shapes (p.234) from green felt, sew them together, and decorate with ricrac trimming and buttons.

Snowman Sew two eyes and draw a carrot nose with fabric pens, then attach a length of wool fabric as a scarf with a button.

Stocking Embroider simple details onto the toe and heel of the sock. Decorate with a folded length of ribbon and a button.

Gingerbread man Sew ricrac trimming onto the arms and feet, and cut out and sew on a scarf and button in festive colours.

Holly and berries Cut two holly shapes (p.233) from tartan fabric, sew them together, insert a wire circle, and add red berry buttons.

Candy cane Wrap a small length of brightly coloured ribbon around the stick and secure it in place with a sewn-on button.

Scent a room

Delicately scented rooms are somehow more inviting, and the subtly uplifting aroma of a pot pourri will make your home seem cosier. Collect a mixture of natural materials and aromatic spices, arrange them in your favourite bowl, and sprinkle over scented oils: the pot pourri will look and smell lovely.

Pot pourri recipes

Spice pot pourri

Collect a few cinnamon sticks, star anise, a nutmeg or two, some cloves, and a selection of dried natural materials or some walnuts and hazelnuts. Sprinkle over 10 drops of cinnamon oil and 5 drops of clove oil.

Citrus pot pourri

Dry some whole clementines, kumquats, orange and lemon slices, and orange and lemon peel. Sprinkle over 10 drops of orange oil and 5 drops of lemon oil.

Pine pot pourri

Collect the cones and a few small branches of any fragrant evergreens – pine, juniper, cypress, and so on. Sprinkle over 10 drops of pine oil and 5 drops of cedar oil.

Garden pot pourri

Gather a selection of natural materials such as thistles, teasels, berries, rosehips, and lavender and rosemary stems, and allow them to dry out thoroughly. Sprinkle over 10 drops of lavender oil and 5 drops of rosemary oil.

Pot pourri is made of three ingredients: dried natural materials, which comprise the filling, and spices and scented oils to create fragrance. The natural materials can include whatever you find visually pleasing and suit the type of pot pourri you're making. Collect interesting seasonal flowers, seed heads, flower heads, fruits, sprigs of foliage, and berries. To dry these ingredients thoroughly, spread them in a single layer on newspaper and leave for a week or so in a warm, dry place out of the sun and away from draughts. Fruits such as oranges, lemons, and kumquats need to be dried slightly differently: cover a wire rack with muslin, place the whole fruits or fruit slices in a single layer on top and leave in the oven on a low temperature or in a cabinet for up to 48 hours.

Making up a pot pourri

Arrange the dried natural materials and spices in a large bowl and sprinkle a few drops of scented essential oil over them. Cover the pot pourri in the bowl until needed and refresh with a few more drops of oil when necessary. Try mixing your own combination of scented oils to create a pleasing aroma, or follow a recipe (left).

Scenting a room quickly

Other, quicker ways of creating scent include placing pine cones, orange peel, or seasoned apple wood on top of a wood fire as it burns, and placing a saucer of orange peel or lemon peel, or small bowls of water containing a few drops of scented oil, next to a warm radiator.

Floral craft techniques

Working with natural foliage provides the perfect excuse to go for a walk in your local park, woodland, or forest – or you may even find suitable greenery in your garden. Look out for items that have fallen from trees, such as pine cones and acorns. Using fresh cuttings of berries and firs creates a lovely seasonal aroma, or you can enhance the natural fragrance with a few drops of an appropriate fragrance oil.

Making a wreath frame

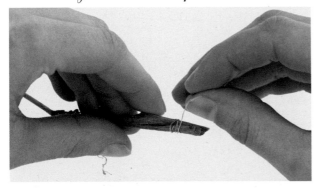

1 Strip two equal lengths of vine of their leaves. Secure them together by binding with a short length of fine wire.

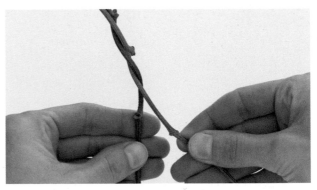

2 Twist the vines together to make one strong length. Secure the other end with wire.

3 Bring the two ends together to create a circle. Twist the ends around each other and tie them together with a short length of wire. If the vines are too long, overlap the ends; if they're too short, introduce an additional length.

4 To strengthen the frame, add more lengths of stripped vine. Tie one end to the frame with wire and wind the vine around the frame, securing the other end with wire. Repeat until you have a strong, firm frame.

5 To keep the shape even and strengthen the frame more, tie small pieces of wire at regular intervals around the frame.

Working with fresh foliage

1 Ensure each stem of foliage is fresh, clean, and dry, and that it looks healthy. Avoid using materials that are mouldy, as the mould may spread.

2 Use a sharp pair of scissors to trim foliage to the required size. For thick stems, use a pair of pruning shears. These speciality gardening scissors can cut through branches up to 2cm (¾in) thick.

Making fir bunches

Use a sharp pair of scissors to trim the sprigs of fir to 4cm (1½in) lengths. Take small bunches of fir (about five sprigs) and wind a length of wire around the bottom of their stems to hold them together.

Securing foliage to the frame

1 To secure fresh foliage such as fir bunches to the frame, use a short length of wire to wrap the base of the bunch to the frame.

2 Use superglue to attach dried foliage, cones, and other materials. Apply a dot of glue to the base of the item and then press in place, making sure not to glue any other foliage together.

Keeping foliage fresh

Fresh foliage should last throughout the winter season, though it will wilt more quickly if it is left outdoors without shelter from the wind. Spritz it regularly with a fine mist of water to keep it fresh.

Enhancing the fragrance

If you wish, you can add a few drops of an appropriate fragrance oil to fresh or dried foliage to enhance the scent of your festive wreath.

Winter wreath

Wreaths are a great introduction to floristry, giving you a chance to work with both fresh and dried foliage. Here, bunches of fir create the base for the frame, and pine cones, acorns, and colourful berries are dotted around to add texture and colour. You could also add leaves, dried fruits, and nuts to create a festive design that is unique and smells gorgeous.

Materials

- Stripped vine stems
- Selection of fresh foliage (fir sprigs, myrtle, berries, eucalyptus leaves)
- Selection of dried foliage (pine cones, acorns)
- Fragrance oil (optional)
- Hook or ribbon

Equipment

- Fine wire
- Scissors or garden secateurs
- Measuring tape
- Superglue
- Spray bottle

1 Use the vine stems to create a circular frame, approximately 30cm (12in) in diameter (see Making a wreath frame, p.22). Around six rounds of vine, secured with wire, will make a thick, sturdy frame.

2 Prepare 15–20 fir bunches (see Making fir bunches, p.23). Attach each one to the frame with wire so that they face the same direction. Overlap one bunch with the next to cover the entire frame.

3 Trim the remaining fresh foliage to size and arrange it around the wreath. Play with the design until you are happy with it before securing the foliage in place. Use a measuring tape to check that the spacing between the foliage is even.

4 Tuck individual sprigs of fresh foliage into the frame between the fir bunches. Attach other bunches of foliage with short lengths of wire, tucking the ends of the wire into the fir to hide them.

5 Arrange the dried foliage on top of the wreath to get an idea of the finished look, then glue in position.

6 Hang the wreath on a hook, or if you prefer, attach a ribbon at the top to hang it. You can scent it with a few drops of fragrance oil or leave it as it is. Spritz regularly with water to keep it fresh.

Foliage and berry wreath

This lovely, natural-looking wired wreath of complementary and harmonious colours includes some dyed leaves to give the best effect: the dye almost preserves the fresh leaves so they don't turn dry and brittle (although if they get wet they can stain paintwork). The base of the wreath is built up with moss, which is a better option than floral foam, as it is lighter and has more depth at the side to attach the foliage. Turn the wire frame around as you pack in the moss so that the section you work on is always in front of you. Either hang the wreath, unadorned, on a wall or propped up on a mantelpiece, or attach a bow and hang it on a door. You can also lay it flat in the middle of a table and place a candle in the centre. It should last for two weeks.

Flowers and foliage

- 12 dyed beech stems
- 4 dyed eucalyptus stems
- 12 miniature hebe stems
- 12 dyed oak leaf stems
- 8 pepper berry sprays
- 1 large bag sphagnum moss
- 8 unripe blackberry sprays
- 12 rosemary sprigs

Equipment

- Wire wreath frame, 30cm (12in) in diameter
- Florist's scissors
- 1 ball of garden string
- 22 gauge wire
- Ribbon (optional)

1 Prepare the foliage (see p.23): cut the stems down to 12–15cm (5–6in) or so and strip the leaves off the lower 2.5cm (1in) of each stem.

2 Position the wire frame so the larger ring lies below the smaller ring. Tie the string onto the frame at any point and secure it in a knot. Take a large handful of moss, tease it apart slightly, and pack it between the two rings in a rounded shape. Gather up loose ends as you press the moss into place, then wind the string diagonally around it to keep it in place. Repeat until the frame is covered.

3 Trim the moss with scissors. Cut the string, leaving a length of about 40cm (16in) still attached to the wreath. Make a loop in the string 10cm (4in) from the attached end. Hold the loop in one hand and the tail end in the other and cross them over under the wreath. Bring them back up above the wreath and tie them in a knot. Trim the loose ends.

4 If you want to hang the finished wreath, feel for the edge of the frame and insert a length of thick wire into the moss, under the frame at an angle, and out the other side. Bring the ends together to make a loop and twist one end around the other. Trim and hide the twisted ends inside the moss. Holding the loop, twist the wreath around twice in the same direction to tighten the base of the loop.

5 Tie the ball of string back onto the wreath at any point. Place three to four beech leaf stems on top of the moss and wrap string tightly over the stems to secure them to the wreath. Turn the wreath around slightly and place a stem of hebe partly over the leaves to create a staggered effect. Secure it in place with the string.

6 Add each piece of foliage in turn, placing small bunches on the sides and top of the moss. Stagger each group of foliage and turn the wreath as you work.

7 When you have added enough foliage to give a well-balanced look, tie off the string in the same way as before: make a double loop, tuck one loop under the wreath, and tie the two single loops together securely.

8 If you spot any gaps in the wreath, or it looks slightly unbalanced in parts, tuck a few pieces of woody-stemmed foliage, such as rosemary and hebe, in under the string to even it out. Tie the ribbon in a bow and attach it to the frame, if using.

Mixed winter arrangement

This crisp white and green vase arrangement, with its heavy winter berries, is warmed up gently by exotic cymbidium orchids (these orchids flower on a very long stem, so the individual heads can be cut off and inserted into orchid vials to give them enough height to suit the design). Such an elegant, festive display would look stunning in a hallway, master bedroom, on a dining room table, or on a low coffee table. The soft-stemmed anemones may need replacing after a few days, but the other blooms should last up to 10 days if you keep them in good condition.

1 Place the chicken wire inside the vase and fill the vase with water.

2 Arrange the skimmia stems first. Keep turning the vase around as you add the foliage to create a fully three-dimensional domed effect. Try not to add too much foliage at this stage.

3 Add the single roses next, placing the shorter stems around the edge of the arrangement and longer ones near the centre to reinforce the domed effect. The flowers should look ordered and not muddled. Keep turning the vase so it faces you as you add the roses.

4 Arrange the hypericum and spray roses next, spacing them evenly throughout the arrangement. Recess the flowers slightly so that the tips of the skimmia leaves break the curved contours of the blooms. Then add the anemones.

5 Finally, add the cymbidium orchids. They can be quite dominant in a floral display, so it's worth arranging them last to work out where they sit best.

Flowers and foliage

- 6 white spray roses
- 5 cymbidium orchids
- 6 single white roses
- 10 hypericum berry stems
- 6 white anemones
- 10 skimmia stems

Equipment

- Opaque green glazed flared vase, around 19cm (7in) high
- Chicken wire
- Florist's scissors

Possible substitutions

Trachelium (for anemonies), mini amaryllis (for spray roses), Singapore orchids (for cymbidium orchids), berried ivy and rosemary (for skimmia)

Winter bouquet

We tend to assume that winter is bereft of plants with colour and variety, but this beautiful mixed hand-tied bouquet uses species such as berried ivy as a feature rather than as a backdrop to give structure, definition, and interest. This bouquet is ideal as a gift or as a table centrepiece in a clear glass vase at a dinner party. It will last up to ten days in water if you refresh the water and re-cut the stems.

1 Sort the different ingredients into separate piles. Hold one amaryllis stem gently upright in one hand and encircle it with two or three stems of berried ivy.

2 Add a rose and twist the bunched blooms around slightly in your hand, then add a stem of hypericum. Keep the stems spiralled by adding them all at the same angle and turning the arrangement in the same direction as you work.

3 When you have added one of each of all the different ingredients, check that you are happy with the arrangement of stems by tilting it towards you, or checking it in a mirror. Trim the stems if necessary if the bouquet is becoming unwieldy in your hand. Add another amaryllis stem at an angle and continue to add the rest of the flowers and foliage.

4 Tie the arrangement securely with a length of raffia or garden string. Treat the amaryllis stems with care, as they may split under too much pressure.

5 Cut the stems at an angle so they are roughly the same length and will all be able to sit in water. If the arrangement is well balanced, it should be able to stand unaided. If the bouquet is a gift to someone, stand it in water until you present it.

Flowers and foliage

- 5 ruby red single roses
- 7 'Red Lion' amaryllis
- 5 'Tamango' spray roses
- 7 'Dolly Parton' hypericum stems
- 10 berried ivy stems

Equipment

- Florist's scissors
- Raffia or garden string

Tip

Amaryllis stems are fragile and the flower heads they carry are heavy, so the stems can easily split if you hold them too tightly. Buy stems that are as fresh as possible with the buds just opening so the flower heads don't splay out in the arrangement.

Evergreen centrepiece

A special seasonal foliage centrepiece will dress your table perfectly and set the scene for a festive meal. Evergreen foliage such as bay and conifer will last well and look fresher for longer than some other seasonal varieties, but choose whatever you have available in the garden, or can buy, to make the best-looking table display.

1 Place the baking dish on a flat, level surface. Use a dish with a fixed, rather than a removable, base, so that water won't leak out of it.

2 Position the candle in the centre of the dish. If you wish, you can stick the candle into place, but use a waterproof glue to do this.

Materials

• Deep, fluted baking dish

• 1 large candle

• Waterproof glue (optional)

• Small bunches of evergreen foliage, such as bay and conifer

• A few pine cones

Equipment

• Secateurs

• Thin garden wire

3 Cut the conifer foliage into small bundles using secateurs. Tie wire around each bundle and place them in the dish around the candle.

4 Insert other foliage in between the conifer bundles. Position the pine cones around the candle and add a little water to keep the foliage fresh.

Herb variation

Gather a selection of fresh, seasonal herbs such as rosemary, sage, thyme, and bay leaves, and use them to create an alternative table centrepiece (pp.34–35).

Fresh foliage variation
Pick a selection of whatever fresh foliage and winter flowers you may have growing in your winter garden for this variation on the evergreen centrepiece (pp.34–35).

Individual setting variations

Rosemary and sage Place a few sprigs of rosemary in a tiny galvanized bucket, tuck in a sage stem, and add a little water.

Bay leaf, thyme, and rosemary Place thyme and rosemary sprigs in a tiny bucket and insert three bay leaves in a row.

Ivy and red berries Fill an egg cup with sprigs of bright red berries and tuck in a few short lengths of ivy around the edge.

Rosehips, ivy, and moss Put a few slightly longer rosehip stems in an egg cup and pack moss and ivy leaves around them.

Fresh flowers Cut fresh flowers from plants that flourish in a winter garden, such as Christmas rose (*Helleborus niger*), Lenten rose (*Helleborus orientalis*), or witch hazel (*Hamamellis mollis*). Put them in a small foil-lined box or pot, and add a little water.

Grow a mistletoe shrub

The evergreen mistletoe plant has become an essential part of our Christmas tradition, and everyone loves its romantic connotations. The bushy shrub is actually a partial parasite that grows in the branches of old trees: it extracts essential nutrients and water by pushing its roots under the bark of the host tree. Although it is slow-growing and can be hard to establish, mistletoe is worth cultivating if you enjoy its clusters of smooth, bright green, oval leaves and waxy white berries in your home at Christmas time.

Mistletoe (*Viscum album*) reproduces naturally when birds – usually mistle thrushes – eat the berries and excrete the seeds onto the bark of a host tree, where they germinate. Popular host trees are those with soft bark, particularly apple trees, and also hawthorn, lime, and poplar trees. After attaching itself to the host, a young plant produces leaves after the first year; just two new branches with a pair of leaves at each tip grow every year.

Propagating mistletoe

The best time to propagate mistletoe is between March and April, when the seeds are fully ripe. If you can't find fresh berries from a living plant, preserve some Christmas sprigs with berries in a jar of water in the window of a cold, frost-free room until the end of February. Use the sticky "glue" of the berry to attach it to the side or underside of an apple tree branch about 20cm (8in) in diameter. The higher up a tree the branch is, and the more sunlight the plant gets, the better. Wind some wool or twine around the branch to mark the site and leave the plant to establish naturally. It's worth applying 15 or more berries to your host tree, as mistletoe requires male and female plants to produce berries. The germination rate is also quite low (only one in ten seeds becomes a plant), and some berries may fall off or be eaten by birds. It will take four to five years for the plant to produce berries.

To decorate your home with mistletoe, cut a few stems from the shrub with a pair of shears, bind the base of the stems with some twine, and hang the bundle from a ceiling light or above a doorway.

Edible bird decorations

A garden full of wildlife is always an uplifting sight on a winter's day. To encourage birds into your garden, hang homemade bird-seed balls from trees and shrubs. The birds rely on these additional sources of nutrients if natural foods are scarce and in severe winter weather when snow is on the ground. Use a recycled glass tumbler as a mould if you don't have an old tennis ball.

Materials

- 500g (1lb 2oz) lard
- 100g (3½oz) coarse oats
- 100g (3½oz) nuts – peanuts are a good choice
- 100g (3½oz) dried fruits
- 100g (3½oz) seeds – sunflower seeds are the best choice
- Garden wire
- Old tennis ball or similar, sliced in half and with a small round hole cut out of the top, then resealed by wrapping a length of wire around the ball and twisting the wire ends together securely
- Garden string

1 Put the lard into a saucepan and melt it gently over a low heat. While the lard is melting, mix the dry ingredients together.

2 Add handfuls of the dry food to the melted lard and mix them together. The dry ingredients should all be well coated in the lard.

3 Insert a looped piece of wire, a little longer than the mould, down through the centre of the mould. Pack the seed mix in around the wire.

4 Leave the seed mix in the moulds to cool completely, then remove the moulds, attach string to the wires, and hang the decorations up high.

Buy and recycle a real tree

For many of us, a real tree dressed with decorations is what Christmas is all about, and it takes pride of place in our homes. Looking after a cut Christmas tree properly will help to prolong its fresh scent and vibrant colour, but just as important is knowing how to recycle the tree afterwards, because the benefits of recycling Christmas trees are enormous.

It takes tree farmers about ten years to produce a 3m (10ft) Christmas tree, and some varieties can reach great heights if left to grow: the Nordman fir (*Abies nordmanniana*) can reach 40m (13ft), for example. The best varieties to choose are Noble fir (*Abies procera*) and Nordman fir (*Abies nordmanniana*), since they have a good colour and scent and hang on to their needles well, and Scots pine (*Pinus sylvestris*), which has the best scent.

Choosing a tree

Buy a locally grown tree with a Christmas tree growers' association label to ensure it has been sustainably grown: you'll be supporting your local grower and minimizing the impact of transport miles, and you can guarantee it has been freshly cut and its needles will stay on longer. Norway Spruce (*Picea abies*), the "original" Christmas tree, is mostly imported from Scandinavia and Holland and is cut down weeks before you buy it, which is why it sheds its needles quickly. Cut 5–12mm (⅛–½in) off the base of your tree trunk, stand it in water, add a tablespoon of honey (to mimic the tree's sap), and keep the room as cool as possible to help the tree stay fresher for longer.

Recycling your tree

The UK currently sends almost all cut trees to landfill sites, but recycled trees can be reduced to chippings and used to benefit the environment again as mulch, path surfacing, and soil improvers. Most councils now provide a collection point from which the trees will be properly pulped and recycled, or you can search online to find out where your nearest recycling centre is.

Christmas tree facts

According to the charity Action for Sustainable Living, more than six million cut trees were bought last year in the UK, but only 750,000 – about 12.5 per cent – were recycled. The rest created 9,000 tonnes of waste in landfill sites, and will take hundreds of years to biodegrade.

In past years, many trees were flown from elsewhere in Europe into the UK, but today a large number of trees are grown in British plantations. Approximately 12,000 hectares of land yield eight million trees each year.

When buying a tree, check that it has the BCTGA (British Christmas Tree Growers Association) logo, which guarantees that is has been sustainably farmed.

An artificial Christmas tree may be reusable, but it will probably have been made from a petroleum-based product and may well have been flown in from China. The materials commonly used in the manufacture of artificial trees are PVC, polyurethane foam, and steel. Although you may reuse it for several years, if your tree is not recyclable it will eventually linger for centuries in a landfill site.

Christmas tree in a pot

One of the great pleasures of Christmas is decorating a real tree, so why not buy a living tree with roots and plant it in a pot? A small tree makes a great table decoration. You can re-pot it, care for it through the seasons, and reuse it for several Christmases to come. Ideally, buy a container-grown tree with a Forest Stewardship Council (FSC) accreditation from a small-scale sustainable grower.

Materials

- 1 dwarf conifer tree with the roots well soaked in a bucket of water; if you choose another variety, check on the eventual height of the tree before you buy it
- 1 container with draining holes
- Bark-based, coarse organic compost
- Watering can

Tip

Owning a living tree
Don't keep the tree indoors for any longer than one month: the warmth and light may encourage it to break dormancy. Feed and water it regularly, re-pot into a larger container in early spring, and add some slow-release organic fertilizer, such as comfrey pellets.

1 Tease the roots of the root ball to loosen them. Fill the base of the container with some compost and place the tree in the container.

2 Pack the spaces around the root ball with more compost. Gently shake the container occasionally to distribute the compost evenly.

3 Fill the container to just below the rim with some more compost, then firm the earth around the plant with your hands.

4 Water the plant thoroughly to ensure that all the compost is wet, allow to drain, and then bring it indoors to decorate.

Homemade Christmas tree decorations

These delightful decorations are all made from eco-friendly materials, such as vintage fabric (pp.56–59), recycled materials (pp.50–51), and discarded paper (pp.54–55), and are all endlessly reusable.

A flock of festive birds

These beautiful felt tree decorations are fun to make and last a lifetime. The basic method is straightforward; it's up to you how sophisticated you want the decorations and details to be. Take your inspiration from your favourite birds, and make these felt creations as colourful as you like. Make them uniquely personal by adding a family member's initials to each finished decoration.

1 Cut two body and wing shapes and some flower and leaf shapes for each bird. Make a hole in the top of each body shape with a skewer.

2 Stitch a flower eye onto the outside of each body shape at the head, then sew some flower and leaf motifs onto the body and wings.

3 Embroider and decorate the felt shapes, then sew the two body shapes together using blanket stitch. Repeat with the two wing shapes.

4 Cut a slit close to the top of the bird's body and push through the wings. Thread the leather strip through the slit and tie it in a loop.

Materials

- Felt in assorted colours
- Festive bird templates (pp.238–39)
- Scissors
- Skewer
- Coloured embroidery thread and needle
- Found and recycled materials to decorate the bird (optional, see Tip)
- Leather strips or lengths of twine

Tip

Recycled decorations
Source a variety of items from the garden or kitchen shelves or drawers to decorate each bird. Look out for grasses, twigs, dried flowers, dried pulses, rice and pasta, bay leaves, old sweet wrappers, buttons, and vintage beads.

Festive bird variations

Decorate these exquisite birds in flight with whatever foraged materials you can find: glue on a few grass heads, twigs, or thin ribbons to create plumage, or sew on some recycled sequins or vintage beads to make the birds sparkle as they catch the light.

Recycled paper decorations

It's worth collecting all sorts of attractive or colourful recycled papers to make these child-friendly tree decorations. Look out for wallpaper samples, pages from magazines, and old oddments of wrapping paper, and recycle the cardboard from items such as tea and cereal boxes to use as the backing material for each decoration.

Materials

For each decoration

- Template (pp.240–43)
- Recycled paper in festive colours
- Recycled cardboard
- Eco-friendly adhesive glue
- Scissors
- Length of string or wool
- 1 vintage bead or button

Tip

Eco decorations

It's worth making your own tree decorations, as bought decorations are often chemically treated, or made from non-biodegradable substances.

1 Place the template on the piece of paper and draw around it. Cut out a piece of cardboard roughly the same size as the piece of paper.

2 Glue the piece of recycled cardboard onto the back of the paper and leave to one side for a while for the glue to dry completely.

3 Cut out the paper shape neatly using a sharp pair of scissors. Trim the shape if necessary so that no pen or pencil marks are showing.

4 Thread both ends of the string through a bead or button to create a loop. Glue the string loop to the back of the card and allow to dry.

Scented fabric hearts

These pretty little filled fabric hearts look adorable hanging from a tree, but they can also be given as stocking fillers to be hung in wardrobes or tucked into drawers to fragrance clothes. Dried lavender flowers or natural pot pourri both make ideal fillings, or fill the hearts with grains of dried rice or barley fragranced with a few drops of your favourite scented essential oil.

1 Using the template, cut out two heart shapes from the fabric. Align and sew them together around the edges, leaving a small gap on one side.

2 Snip gently around the edges of the seams with the scissors, taking care not to cut the stitching. Then turn the fabric inside out.

3 Iron the fabric to get rid of any creases, then pack the heart with the scented filling. Sew up the open gap with the needle and thread.

4 Make a knot at one end of the string and sew it onto the heart. Thread the string through the stick and leaves, knot it, and finish in a loop.

Materials

- Heart template (p.236)
- Recycled fabric (use an old gingham tea towel or tablecloth)
- Scissors or pinking shears
- Cotton thread and needle
- Iron
- Filling material, such as dried lavender or rice
- 2–3 drops of scented essential oil (optional)
- Length of string
- 1 cinnamon stick with a hole through the centre (use a knitting needle or skewer to do this)
- Several dried bay leaves with a hole through the centre of each

Advent calendar sacks

If you want a change from the traditional, flat card Advent calendars, try making these fabric sacks to hang on your Christmas tree, or use them to decorate a smaller table-top tree. They are easy to make, and can be filled with whatever treats your family enjoys – try a mixture of homemade sweets, bite-size cookies, fresh nuts, and tiny gifts.

1 Using the template, cut the cloth into 48 sack shapes. Then cut 24 small squares of fabric, each about 3 x 3cm (1¼ x 1¼in) in size.

2 Align two sack shapes, correct sides facing inwards. Sew three sides together. Leave a seam of 1cm (½in). Repeat with the other shapes.

3 Mark a day of Advent, from 1 to 24, on each fabric square. Make a hole in the top corner of each square, thread through the twine, and knot it.

4 Fill each sack with a few treats, then tie the twine around the top to seal the sack. Secure the ends in a loop and hang from the tree.

Materials

- Template (p.244)
- Old tablecloth or pretty curtain material
- Scissors or pinking shears
- Cotton needle and thread or sewing machine
- Eco-friendly fabric pen
- 24 lengths of garden twine or string, each about 32cm (12½in) long
- Treats to fill each sack

Peg doll tree angel

An old-fashioned peg doll has a nostalgic appeal that makes it a perfect decoration for any Christmas tree. If your tree is small, hang the angel right at the top of the tree, or for a larger tree make up several angels to dress the branches. Use a traditional wooden clothes peg to create the angel's body; if you can't buy any of these pegs locally, try finding them on the internet.

Materials

- Recycled natural raffia
- 1 dolly peg
- Eco-friendly adhesive glue
- Eco-friendly marker pen
- Old tablecloth
- Templates (p.237)
- Scissors
- Cotton thread and needle, or sewing machine
- Garden wire, about 15cm (6in) long
- Cream felt (p.16)
- Recycled ribbon

1 Attach a few short strands of raffia to the top of the dolly peg with a dab of glue. Draw two eyes onto the peg head with the marker pen.

2 Cut two shapes from the cloth using the template. Align and sew the sides of the dress together, leaving a gap in the neck to fit the peg.

3 Twist one end of the wire into a circle. Bend the free end at right angles to the circle. Wind it around the peg to secure the halo in place.

4 Cut the wings from the felt using the template. Glue a loop of ribbon, then the dress, onto the wings. Glue the peg inside the dress.

Cinnamon spice bundles

With its distinctly warm, aromatic smell, cinnamon spice can instantly create a familiar festive scent in any room. Golden-red cinnamon sticks, which are actually pieces of bark from the evergreen cinnamon tree, are easy to purchase and make striking natural decorations. Try finding long cinnamon sticks to make these spice bundles for your Christmas tree.

1 Secure the cinnamon sticks in a bundle with the elastic band. Thread the wire under the elastic band and secure it tightly in a loop.

2 Thread a nutmeg onto one end of the raffia. Tie a knot in the end of the raffia to secure the nutmeg. Repeat at the other end.

3 Wrap the raffia around the cinnamon bundle a couple of times so that the elastic band is completely hidden. Secure in a knot.

4 Glue the star anise onto the front of the orange slice, then glue the orange slice onto the raffia so that it covers the knot.

Materials

For each decoration

- 6–8 cinnamon sticks

- 1 recycled elastic band

- Length of thin wire, approximately 15cm (6in) long

- 2 nutmegs with a hole drilled through the centre of each (use a clamp and fine-bore drill bit)

- Length of recycled natural raffia, about 50cm (20in) long

- Eco-friendly adhesive glue

- 1 star anise

- 1 dried orange slice

Spiced orange decorations

Even after they have been dried thoroughly, oranges retain enough of an aroma to fill a room for many days with their citrus scent. Their mellow orange hues and cylindrical shape also mean that they make naturally attractive decorations, especially when hung from the vibrant green branches of a real conifer tree.

Materials

For each decoration

- Eco-friendly adhesive glue
- 1 star anise
- 1 dried orange slice
- 1 flat, dried bay leaf
- Several lengths of thin wire
- A handful of cloves
- 1 dried, whole clementine
- Skewer or knitting needle
- 1 cinnamon stick

Tip

Dehydrating fruits

Arrange the slices and whole fruits in a single layer on a piece of muslin on a wire rack. Leave to dry in a very low oven or a warm airing cupboard, which can take 48 hours or longer.

1 Glue the star anise onto the front of the orange slice, and the bay leaf onto the back. Secure a length of wire in a loop at the top of the orange.

2 Stick cloves into the clementine in a pattern. Push a skewer through the fruit, thread wire through the hole and secure one end in a loop.

3 Thread wire lengthways through the cinnamon stick. Bend one end over, thread the other end through the clementine loop, and secure.

4 Attach the loose wire at the top of the clementine to the orange slice. The three parts should now all be joined together by wire.

Natural decoration variations

Simple orange pomanders Make natural baubles by evenly scoring orange skins and slowly dehydrating the fruits.

Fruit and flower sprigs For simple, stylish decorations, tie stems of rosehips to dried teasle heads with wire and finish with a loop.

Spiced fruits Attach single fruits and dried sliced chillies with coloured wire to either end of a decorated orange slice.

Frosted Christmas lanterns Use a few wispy seed heads instead of a thistle head to give decorations a frosted effect.

Citrus slices Make a hole in the top of a dried orange slice, thread through a length of string, and secure in a knot.

Cinnamon walnut bundles Attach a walnut at either end of thin rope, wrap the rope around the sticks, and glue on a star anise.

Cranberry hearts Thread thin string through dried cranberries using a needle, secure in a heart shape, and finish with a loop.

Snow clouds Tie extra quantites of wispy or fluffy seed heads to Chinese lanterns with thin wire and finish with a loop.

Nougat sweets

These wonderfully sticky, very light soft sweets are perfect for filling tiny galvanized buckets or fabric candy cane cones hanging from the Christmas tree. You'll need a sugar thermometer to ensure that the sugar solution reaches the correct temperature as it boils; be aware that it is extremely hot at this stage, so don't let children come too close to the pan.

Ingredients

- 680g (1½lb) granulated sugar
- 340ml (12fl oz) golden syrup
- 60ml (2fl oz) clear honey
- 235ml (8fl oz) water
- 2 egg whites, beaten in a large bowl, until stiff
- 1 tsp vanilla extract
- 275g (10oz) mixture of blanched almonds, hazelnuts, and macadamia nuts

1 Heat the sugar, syrup, honey, and water in a saucepan until it reaches 154°C (310°F). Stand the thermometer in the pan to check the temperature.

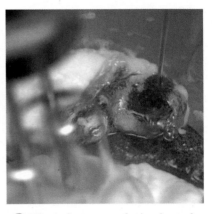

2 When the sugar solution is ready, add it to the bowl of beaten egg whites, beating the mixture constantly until it is stiff and waxy.

3 Add the vanilla extract and the nuts to the bowl and fold them all carefully into the mixture using a large metal spoon.

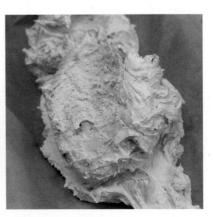

4 Put the nougat mix into a tin lined with greaseproof paper. Allow to cool completely before cutting it into small squares. Store in an airtight tin.

Iced biscuit decorations

This simple gingerbread recipe is easy to follow and makes about 35 edible tree decorations. The dough is easy to handle, so children will love rolling it, cutting out different festive shapes, and decorating the baked biscuits with icing. Once cool, thread a ribbon through each biscuit and hang on the tree.

1 Preheat the oven to 190°C (375°F). Put the flour, bicarbonate of soda, ginger, and cinnamon in a bowl. Rub in the butter so the mix resembles breadcrumbs. Stir in the sugar.

2 Add the egg and syrup, then mix to form a dough. Turn out onto a lightly floured surface and knead to bring the dough together.

3 Divide the dough into two batches. Roll each batch out with a lightly floured rolling pin to an even thickness of about 5mm (¼in).

4 Cut shapes with biscuit cutters, make a hole in each with a skewer, place on greased baking trays, and bake for about 10 minutes.

Ingredients

- 350g (12oz) plain flour
- 1 tsp bicarbonate of soda
- 2 tsp ground ginger
- 2 tsp ground cinnamon
- 100g (4oz) butter, cut into pieces
- 175g (6oz) light muscavado sugar
- 1 egg, beaten
- 4 tbsp golden syrup

For the icing:

Beat 1 egg white with 150–200g (5–7oz) icing sugar (adjust the quantity slightly, depending on the size of the egg; the icing should be smooth).

Iced biscuit variations

Angel Beat the egg white and icing sugar to a smooth consistency. Pipe patterns to suit shapes like this angel.

Star To create repeat patterns like this star shape, ice the outside edge first and echo the shape as you work inwards.

Heart Pipe on these straight and fluted lines with a piping bag or a clean, recycled plastic sandwich bag with the corner cut off.

Shooting star Reopen any holes that close during baking, then pipe icing around them to make patterns like these star shapes.

Holly leaf Press the piping bag gently and evenly with both hands as you draw on intricate details like these holly leaf berries.

Christmas tree Add organic red colouring to a separate batch of icing to make these colour-contrasting tree decorations.

Snowman Change the piping bag nozzle to one with serrated edges for patterned details like the buttons on this snowman.

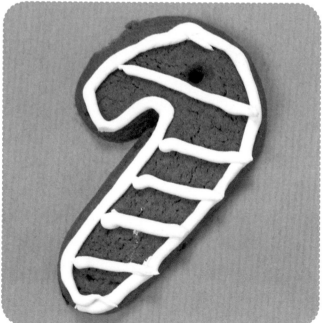

Candy cane Keep the patterns on slim-shaped biscuits clear and simple, such as the outline and stripes on this candy cane.

Painting glass techniques

Glass painting is an inexpensive craft that requires minimal tools and materials. It is a great way to recycle old glassware and give it a new lease of life. Clear glass is the most versatile for painting on, but also consider coloured and frosted glass. Glass paint applied to frosted glass will make it transparent. Practise painting on acetate or an old piece of glass before starting on a project.

Making a template for a straight-sided or conical container

1 Slip a piece of tracing paper inside a straight-sided or conical container. Adjust the paper so that it rests against the glass, then tape it in place. Mark the position of the overlap and the upper edge with a pencil.

2 Remove the tracing paper and cut out the template along the overlap and upper edge. Transfer your design onto the paper with a pen. Stick the paper under the glass with masking tape, butting the side edges of the template together.

Sticking a template under a double curvature

1 Templates to be used on rounded glassware need to be adapted to fit the shape. Make cuts into the template with a pair of scissors.

2 Tape the template under the glass at the top and bottom. The cuts will overlap or spread open to fit the curves of the glassware.

Transferring a design

1 If the aperture is too small to stick a template inside, the design can be transferred to the outer surface of the glass. Turn the tracing over and redraw the lines with a China-graph pencil.

2 Tape the template, Chinagraph-pencil-side down, on the glass. Draw over the lines again with a sharp standard writing pencil to transfer the design onto the glass. Remove the template.

Applying outliner

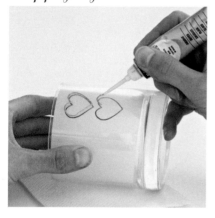

1 Resting the piece on kitchen paper and with the template in place, squeeze the tube of outliner, gently drawing it along the outline of the design. Leave to dry, then turn the piece to continue.

2 Wipe away major mistakes immediately with kitchen paper. When dry, neaten any blobs with a craft knife. Once painted, the viewer's eye will be drawn to the painted areas and not the outliner, so don't overdo the neatening.

Painting on glass

1 Resting the piece on kitchen paper, apply the glass paint generously with a medium paintbrush. Use a fine paintbrush to push the paint into any corners. If working on a curve, keep the glass steady to avoid the paint running to one side.

2 To blend one colour into another, apply both colours to the glass, then mix them together where they meet, making sure that the paint reaches the edge of the outliner. Leave to dry, then turn the glass to continue painting.

Tealight holder

The gentle glow of flickering candlelight never fails to create a cosy atmosphere during a long winter's night. Hand-painted tealight holders can be a charming addition to this display. Keep it simple with red and orange flowers, as shown here, or design your own Christmas motifs. Opt for gold outliner for an elegant and luxurious effect.

Materials

- Straight-sided clear glass tealight holder
- Tracing paper
- Scissors
- Pencil
- Ruler
- Black felt-tip pen
- Masking tape
- Kitchen paper
- Gold outliner
- Piece of white paper
- Orange, red, and yellow transparent glass paints
- Medium and fine artist's paintbrushes

1 Make a template and divide it into fifths. Trace a blossom and leaf motif onto each section 6mm (¼in) below the upper edge with the felt-tip pen. Tape the template inside the tealight holder with masking tape.

2 Resting the tealight holder on its side on kitchen paper, trace the first motif with gold outliner. Leave to dry. Turn the tealight holder and repeat to outline all the motifs. Remove the template when the outliner has dried.

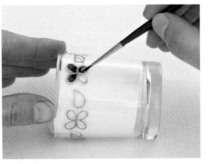

3 Slip a piece of paper inside the tealight holder to show up the area being painted. Apply orange paint to the outer edge of the petals with a medium paintbrush. Apply red paint to the inner edge with a fine paintbrush. Blend the colours and leave to dry.

4 Apply yellow paint to the pointed end of a leaf with a fine paintbrush. Apply orange paint to the rounded end with a medium paintbrush. Blend the colours at the centre of the leaf. Leave to dry, then turn the glass and continue painting.

5 When the last motif is dry, apply a dot of gold outliner at the centre of the flower to neaten it. Apply three tiny dots along the centre of the petals, then five dots along the leaf. Repeat on all the motifs. Leave the outliner to dry.

Glass jar candleholders

This candleholder design uses a jam jar and wire to replicate the appearance of a traditional lantern. Decorate the jars with leaves and seed heads, or other simple decorations, and tie on ribbons that echo the colours of the Christmas decorations in your room. Once lit, don't leave these candles unattended.

Materials

- Several recycled jam jars, baby-food jars, or similiar
- Strong wire
- Selection of leaves and seed heads, either fresh or dried
- Eco-friendly adhesive glue
- Recycled ribbon
- Several tealights

Tip

Recycle old candles
Heat waste candles in a pan over a gentle heat. Lift out the dead wicks and cut a new wick just longer than your mould (try using an old teacup or glass). Soak in the wax. Pour the wax into the lightly oiled mould, ensuring the wick is at the centre. Leave to set.

1 Clean the jars thoroughly and dry them. Put the lids aside. Cut a length of wire just larger than the diameter of the neck of a jar.

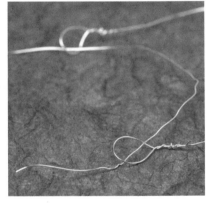

2 Cut a second length of wire about 30cm (12in) long. Make a secure loop at either end. Thread the first length of wire through each loop (see pp.110–11).

3 Wrap the short length of wire around the neck of the jar and secure it tightly. Adjust the loops so that the wire handle works correctly.

4 Glue leaves or seed heads onto the sides of the jar. Tie a ribbon around the neck and slip a tealight into the jar. Decorate the other jars.

Terracotta pot candleholders

Turn three simple terracotta pots into stylish candleholders: line the base of each with recycled kitchen foil, put a beeswax candle in the centre, pack sand around each candle, and cover the sand with a pretty arrangement of fresh foliage and bright berries.

Decorated chair backs

These simple arrangements, made up of a few stems of trailing ivy (*Hedera*), mistletoe (*Viscum album*), and holly (*Ilex*), roughly tied together with natural raffia, and attached to the back of each chair, will lend a lovely rustic detail to your decorated table.

Homemade
Gifts

Soap-making techniques

The basic technique of soap-making involves melting a soap base and re-moulding it into bars or slabs filled with your own custom scents, colours, and additives. Once you have mastered these basics, you can branch out to create highly decorative soaps using techniques such as layering and embedding. The only limit is your imagination.

Preparing the soap base

1 Weigh out enough soap base to fill your moulds, allowing a little extra for wastage. Average-sized bars usually require 80–100g (3–3½oz) of soap. If you're not sure how much soap your mould requires, try cutting a slab to fit it.

2 Use a sharp knife to slice the soap into 2.5cm (1in) chunks. As a rule, the smaller and more regular the pieces, the more quickly and evenly the soap will melt.

Melting the soap base

1 To melt soap on the stove, place it in a heatproof bowl over a pan of simmering water until the soap becomes fully liquid. Stir occasionally, but try to avoid generating air bubbles.

2 Small batches of soap can be melted in the microwave. Place in a microwave-proof bowl and heat on full power in 10-second bursts until it becomes fully liquid. Never boil or overheat the soap; it only has to be warm enough to melt.

Colouring the soap

1 Liquid dyes and pigments should be added in tiny increments to the melted soap. Use the tip of a toothpick to add colour, one drop at a time.

2 If the colour isn't quite strong enough, add a little more dye and stir until it is fully incorporated into the melted soap.

3 Add powdered pigment to a small batch of the melted soap and stir to dissolve it. Then incorporate this with the rest of the melted soap, little by little.

4 For bright, jewel-like colours, mix transparent soap base with liquid dyes or pigments. For flatter, paler shades, use opaque soap base with liquid or powdered colourants.

Scenting the soap

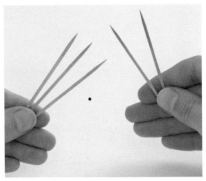

1 Add essential oils and fragrances to the soap just before moulding to minimize evaporation from heat. For small batches, add the oil drop by drop until the aroma is as desired.

2 For larger batches, measure out the fragrance into a beaker. Aim for 2–3 per cent of the total weight of the soap, or 10–15ml (2–3 tsp) per 500g (1lb 2oz) of soap.

3 When blending scents, experiment with top, middle, and base notes. Putting different combinations of dipped toothpicks in a ziplock bag is a good way to play with scent blends.

Enhancing soaps with natural ingredients

1 To add a luxurious, creamy texture to opaque soap, stir in a small portion of a solid moisturizing oil such as shea butter while the soap is melting. Do not exceed 5g (⅕oz) per 100g (3½oz) of soap.

2 For an exfoliating soap, stir in a handful of finely ground oatmeal into the melted soap before moulding. Dried calendula or safflower petals can also be used to create a colourful, mottled texture.

3 For a decorative flourish, place slices of dried citrus fruit in the bottom of the mould and make them adhere by pouring a very thin layer of soap on top. After a minute or two, spritz with rubbing alcohol, then pour in the rest of the soap.

Moulding and storing soap

1 Once all the additives are in place, carefully pour the soap into the moulds. It is common for surface bubbles to appear after pouring; these can be dissolved by spritzing immediately with surgical spirit. Leave to set.

2 After several hours, turn the mould upside down and flex each edge gently to release the soap. If the soap is stubborn, place it in the freezer for 15 minutes and try again. Once unmoulded, slabs can be sliced into bars using a knife or metal scraper.

3 If the soap is not for immediate use, store it in clingfilm to prevent its high glycerine content from attracting humidity in the atmosphere and "sweating".

Layering and embedding

1 It is possible to create bars with multiple colours or scents by pouring in separate layers. Spritz the surface of the soap with surgical spirit immediately after pouring, then leave to set. Spritz again before pouring the next layer.

2 Another popular technique is to embed small pieces of contrasting soap into the centre of the soap bars. These may be anything from simple, hand-cut shapes to decorative centrepieces, created with chocolate moulds or cookie cutters.

3 To create the finished bar, chill the centrepieces in the freezer for at least 30 minutes and then work as you would to layer the soap, placing the centrepieces in the middle layer. Spritz each layer with surgical spirit before pouring the next.

Botanical soap

Have you ever wandered around a craft market and admired the array of rough-cut, rustic-looking, natural soaps that are on offer? You too can produce your very own slab of soothing lavender soap that can be cut up into bars and shared with friends. The same approach can be used with a wide range of dried herbs, flower petals, and essential oils.

Materials

- 25g (scant 1oz) dried lavender buds
- 650g (1lb 7oz) goat's milk soap base, chopped into small pieces
- 15ml (3 tsp) lavender essential oil

Equipment

- Pestle and mortar or food processor
- Heatproof bowl
- Saucepan
- Metal spoon
- Small measuring beaker
- Tupperware container (approx 12.5 x 18cm/ 5 x 7in)
- Metal scraper or knife

1 Divide the lavender buds into two equal portions. Finely grind one of the portions using a pestle and mortar or a food processor. Set aside.

2 Place the soap in a heatproof bowl over a saucepan of simmering water and heat gently. Stir occasionally with a metal spoon until the soap has melted. Remove from the heat.

3 Add the lavender essential oil and the ground lavender and stir constantly for 1–2 minutes. This will help the lavender to remain evenly suspended within the soap. Allow the soap to cool slightly without setting.

4 Pour the mixture into the container. Before the soap starts to form a skin, immediately sprinkle on the unground lavender buds, and press gently with your fingers to help them adhere to the surface.

5 Allow to set for several hours before
unmoulding and slicing into smaller
blocks using a metal scraper or knife.

All-natural luxury soap

Handmade soaps make indulgent gifts, and using the melt-and-pour method they require no specialized skill to make. Create naturally scented and coloured soaps using spices, dried fruits or flowers, essential oils, and soap colourant.

1 Wearing gloves, chop the melt-and-pour soap into pieces and heat in a heatproof bowl over a pan of boiling water, stirring occasionally, until all lumps have melted.

2 Add the desired amount of colouring to the melted soap base and stir until the powder has mixed in and the colour is evenly distributed.

3 Add the lemon peel granules a little at a time, stirring gently. Continue stirring until the granules are spread evenly throughout the soap mixture.

4 Just before you pour the soap mixture into the molud, slowly add the essential oil and stir gently until it is evenly distributed throughout.

Materials

Makes 9 bars

- 1kg (2¼lb) white melt-and-pour soap base
- ¼–¾ tsp yellow natural mineral colour
- Dried lemon peel granules
- Lemon essential oil
- Surgical spirit in a spray bottle
- 9 dried lemon slices
- Cling film

Equipment

- Gloves
- Heatproof bowl
- Pan
- Spatula
- Spoon
- Square mould
- Knife

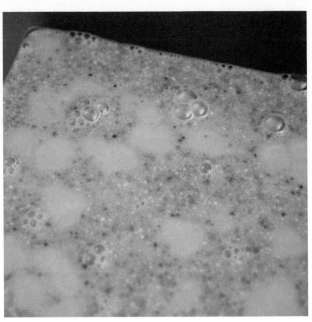

5 Pour approximately three-quarters of the mixture into the mould. Leave the remainder in the bowl over the hot water to keep it melted and warm.

6 Spray the mixture with surgical spirit to remove any bubbles. Let this first layer stand for 20–25 minutes, until it is almost set. It should be hard but warm.

7 Spray the almost-set layer again with surgical spirit. This will act as a glue and help it to bond to the next layer of soap.

8 Slowly pour the remaining mixture into the mould and add the dried lemon slices. You will need to act fast because the top layer will begin to set as soon as it is poured.

9 Create a 3 x 3 pattern so that each bar of soap will contain a lemon slice. Spritz the surface with surgical spirit to remove any bubbles and let it stand until hard.

10 Remove the soap from the mould and cut it with a knife into nine even squares. Wrap each square in cling film to prevent it from attracting moisture.

Soap recipe variations

Bergamot soap ¼–¾ teaspoon orange natural mineral colour, 2¼ teaspoons bergamot essential oil, 9 whole dried orange slices.

Rose soap 2¼ teaspoons rose absolute diluted in 5% grapeseed oil, 100g (3½oz) rose buds.

Cinnamon soap ¼–¾ teaspoon caramel natural mineral colour, 2¼ teaspoons cinnamon leaf essential oil, 9 cinnamon sticks.

Camomile soap ¼–¾ teaspoon green natural mineral colour, 2¼ teaspoons camomile essential oil, 35g (1–1½ oz) dried camomile.

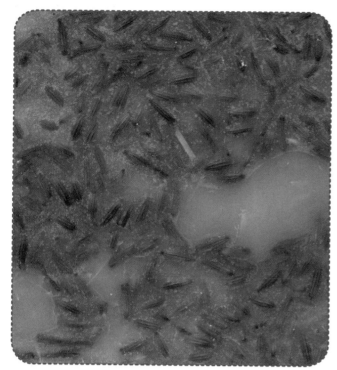

Lavender soap ¼–¾ teaspoon purple natural mineral colour, 2¼ teaspoons English lavender essential oil, 10g (½oz) dried lavender.

Vanilla soap ¼–¾ teaspoon cream soap natural mineral colour, 2¼ teaspoons vanilla essential oil, 3 vanilla pods (use seeds in mixture).

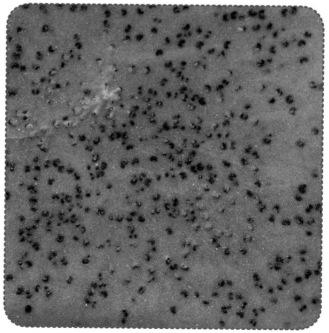

Juniper soap ¼–¾ teaspoon pink natural mineral colour, 2¼ teaspoons juniper essential oil, 100g (4oz) juniper berries.

Sandalwood soap ¼–¾ teaspoon light-brown natural mineral colour, 2¼ teaspoons sandalwood fragrance, 50g (1¾oz) poppy seeds.

Soap variations

Juniper cake-slice soap

You will need

- 1kg (2lb) white melt-and-pour soap base
- ¼ teaspoon pink natural mineral colour
- 2¼ teaspoons juniper essential oil
- 100g (4oz) juniper berries

This soap cake is made like the lemon soap on pp.90–3, but in two stages. First, melt half the soap, adding the pink colour and half the essential oil. Pour it into a round container and let it set, spritzing it with surgical spirit to get rid of any bubbles. Melt the second half of the soap, adding the remaining scent. Spritz the base again, then pour on the second layer of soap. Add the juniper berries to the top, spritzing it one final time to get rid of any remaining bubbles. Once set, remove from the mould and cut into slices.

Moulded vanilla stars

You will need

- 1kg (2lb) white melt-and-pour soap base
- ¼–¾ teaspoon cream natural mineral colour
- 2¼ teaspoons vanilla essential oil
- 3 vanilla pods, cut in pieces

These vanilla-scented stars are made in the same way as the lemon soap (pp.90–93), but the mixture is poured into individual moulds to set. Soap moulds are sold in craft shops, or you can use silicone cake moulds. Vanilla seeds are used instead of lemon peel granules as an exfoliant and for added scent. Vanilla pods can also be used to decorate the tops of the stars by placing them into the mould before the mixture is poured on top.

Cookie-cutter lavender hearts

You will need

- 1kg (2lb) white melt-and-pour soap base
- ¼–¾ teaspoon blue or purple natural mineral colour
- 2¼ teaspoons lavender essential oil
- 10 g (¼ oz) dried lavender

These heart-shaped soaps are made using the same method and quantity of ingredients as the lemon soap on pp.90–93, swapping in the ingredients above. However, instead of cutting the soap into squares, they are cut with heart-shaped cookie cutters. The lavender buds will float to the top, creating an exfoliating layer.

See-through orange soap

You will need

- 1kg (2lb) clear melt-and-pour soap base
- 2¼ teaspoons bergamot essential oil
- 9 dried orange slices

Although made in the same way as the lemon soap on pp.90–93, using a clear soap base and adding a dried orange slice inside the soap gives these soaps a fresh look. Make them by first melting half of the clear soap base and adding half of the essential oil. Pour the mixture into a square mould, then add the orange slices evenly to the top. Allow this layer to set before melting the remaining half of the soap base and adding the remaining essential oil. Spritz the set layer with surgical spirit and add the melted soap mixture to the top. Spritz again to get rid of any bubbles and allow to set. Cut the soap into nine square bars.

Fizzy bath bombs

Bath bombs are solid balls that fizz and bubble as they dissolve, adding scent and colour to the bath water. They make wonderful gifts and are surprisingly easy to make with ingredients that are readily available in most supermarkets.

1 Measure the bicarbonate of soda and sift it into the medium-sized mixing bowl.

2 Add the citric acid to the bicarbonate of soda and mix well with your fingers until fully combined.

3 Split the mixture between the two smaller bowls. Add the colour to the first bowl and mix well with a spoon or your fingers, ensuring that no lumps remain.

4 Add approximately half the fragrance to the first bowl and half to the second bowl. Mix each bowl well, again making sure that no lumps remain.

Materials

Makes 1 bath bomb

- 155g (5½oz) bicarbonate of soda
- 75g (2½oz) citric acid
- ¼ teaspoon purple natural mineral colour
- ½ teaspoon juniper essential oil
- Water in a spray bottle

Equipment

- Sieve
- 1 medium-sized mixing bowl
- 2 small mixing bowls
- Spoon
- Bath bomb mould

5 Spray both bowls lightly with water and mix it in evenly with your fingers. Continue to spritz and mix until the mixture feels damp but not too moist.

6 Fill one of the mould halves halfway with the purple mixture. Gently press the mixture down into the mould with your fingers to remove any pockets of air.

7 Add white mixture to the mould half, leaving a mound at the top. Repeat the process for the other mould half, this time starting with the white mixture.

![Bath bomb mould halves being brought together]

8 Bring the two mould halves together, making sure that the two halves of the bath bomb are lined up exactly. Press the halves together.

9 Leave the bath bomb to set for approximately five minutes. Try not to move it at all during this time because it can be very fragile before it is set.

10 Once set, first remove one of the mould halves. Then place your palm over the bath bomb and gently turn it over. Remove the other mould half.

Organic bath oil

This simple yet luxurious bath oil recipe can be easily adapted to be either relaxing, soothing, or invigorating. Make sure to use organic essential oils. Package the bottled oils in a recycled box lined with coloured tissue papers and include some of the ingredients for a rustic finish, or simply tie a length of vintage ribbon around the neck of each bottle.

Materials

- 50ml (2fl oz) sweet almond oil

For Relaxing bath oil

- 10 drops of sandalwood essential oil
- 5 drops of jasmine essential oil
- 5 drops of orange essential oil

For Soothing bath oil

- 10 drops of rose essential oil
- 5 drops of chamomile essential oil
- 5 drops of lavender essential oil

For Invigorating bath oil

- 10 drops of grapefruit essential oil
- 5 drops of lemon essential oil
- 5 drops of juniper essential oi

Equipment

- 1 pretty recycled bottle and lid, sterilized
- Measuring cup
- 1 label

1 Carefully decant the almond oil from a measuring cup into the sterilized bottle.

2 Add each of the different essential oils, drop by drop, to the almond oil in the bottle.

3 Screw on the lid firmly and shake the bottle until the ingredients are well blended.

4 Attach a label identifying the oil, and with instructions to add 1 tablespoon of the oil to a warm bath.

Silver clay jewellery

Make beautiful silver jewellery items easily with silver clay.
Available from craft shops, silver clay is 99% silver. When fired with
a kitchen torch, the clay burns off, leaving behind a fully silver item.

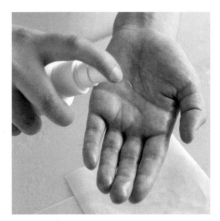

1 Cut out a square of greaseproof paper or use a Teflon mat. Prepare your work surface by applying a small amount of oil over the paper or mat, your hands, and the rolling pin.

2 Place two stacks of four playing cards, each about 5cm (2in) away from each other to act as rolling guides. Soften the clay in your hands and roll it flat.

3 Lift up the rolled clay carefully and place a leaf underneath and on top of it as shown, making sure you line up the stems and tips of the leaves. Roll over the clay again to imprint both sides.

4 Carefully remove the leaves, and lay the clay on a cutting mat or cutting board. Using the craft knife and the template from p.245, carefully cut a leaf shape from the clay.

Materials

- Oil (cooking spray is ideal)
- 7g (¼oz) silver clay
- Real leaves or leaf skeletons
- Silver jump ring

Equipment

- Greaseproof paper or Teflon mat
- Small rolling pin or piece of pipe
- Playing cards
- Craft knife
- Small straw
- Wet and dry sandpaper (600 grit) or sanding pad (220 grit)
- Kitchen blowtorch
- Firing brick or ceramic tile
- Timer
- Tweezers
- Soft wire brush
- 2 pairs of pliers

5 Using the straw, make a hole in the leaf about 5mm (¼in) from the top. This needs to be big enough for your jump ring, bearing in mind that the clay may shrink by up to 10% when fired.

6 Let the clay dry overnight, or, to speed up the process, use a hairdryer or put the clay in an oven at 150°C (300°F) for 10 minutes. Once dry, sand it very carefully to smooth the edges.

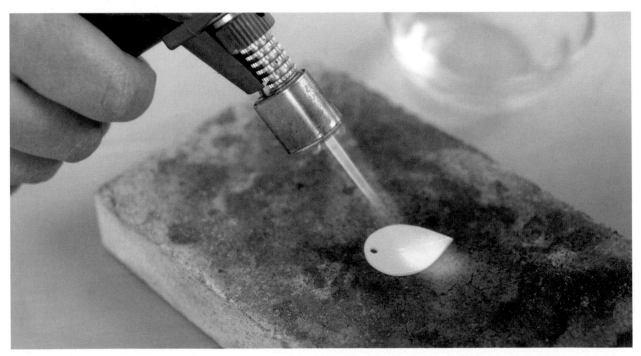

7 Place the leaf on the firing brick or tile in a dimly lit, well ventilated room. Hold the torch 5cm (2in) from the clay and move the flame evenly over it. The leaf will start to glow a peachy orange colour.

8 Once the leaf begins to glow, set the timer for two minutes. If the leaf turns bright red or shiny silver, it is too hot – move the flame away. Once fired, pick up the leaf with tweezers and quench it in water.

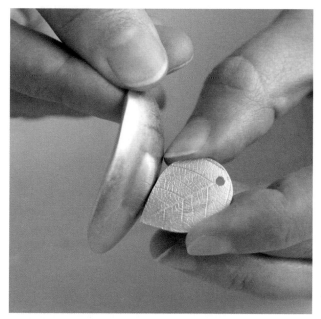

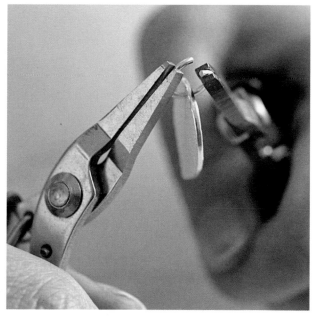

9 The leaf will now be a matte-white colour, even though it is pure silver. Gently brush it with a soft wire brush to reveal the silver colour. To achieve a high shine, rub with the back of a metal spoon.

10 Using two pairs of pliers, gently twist the ends of the jump ring away from each other. Thread it through the hole in your leaf, and then twist the jump ring closed.

Silver jewellery variations

Wallpaper earrings

Patterned wallpaper can be ideal for texturing metal clays, and the variety of designs available is huge. Make these earrings using the same technique as for the silver leaf pendant on pp.104–7, using 15g (½oz) of silver clay. Using the wallpaper, roll and texture your clay as before. Cut ovals from the clay approximately 3cm (1¼in) in length using the template on p.245 and pierce at the top with your straw. Dry out, and torch fire. Burnish for a high shine, and attach ear wires.

Simple button cufflinks

A wide array of textured paper is available from most craft stores; a snakeskin pattern has been used to create these cufflinks made according to the same technique as the silver leaf pendant on pp.104–7 and using the template on p.245. To make, roll out and texture approximately 20g (¾oz) of silver clay. Carefully cut out two discs measuring 2cm (¾in) in diameter, and another two of 1.5cm (⅝in) in diameter. Pierce each of these discs twice using a toothpick (the holes should be positioned to resemble the holes in a button). Dry out and fire the clay as for the silver leaf pendant. Burnish for a high shine, then, using a needle and silver thread, sew the silver clay buttons onto a cufflink chain: 1.5–2cm (⅝–¾in) of chain with roughly 5mm (¼in) links is ideal. Tie off the thread, and use a tiny dot of superglue to ensure the end doesn't come loose.

Leaf bracelet

This simple leaf bracelet requires approximately 25g (1oz) of silver clay. Roll and texture your clay as for the silver leaf pendant on pp.104–7. Then cut out seven pointed ellipses 2.5cm (1in) in length. Pierce each end of the ellipses with your straw. While the pieces of clay are still soft, lay them over a rolling pin to give them a curved shape. Let them dry, and then torch fire as before. Link the elements together using jump rings. Finally, attach a simple clasp.

Lace heart key ring

Fabrics, in particular lace, can be used to produce beautifully delicate patterns in metal clays. To make this heart key ring in the same way as the silver leaf pendant on pp.104–7, roll out approximately 10g (⅜oz) of silver clay. Texture it using lace, and then cut out a heart shape 3.5cm (1⅜in) in length using the template on p.245. Pierce the top of the heart with your straw. Dry out and fire the clay, then burnish to a high shine. Use a jump ring to attach the heart to a key ring and chain.

Wirework techniques

There are many different types of wire. If you are new to wirework, copper wire is very good material because it is malleable. Many craft shops stock wire in a range of coloured finishes, and coat hanger wire is ideal when a strong structure is required. Household pliers can be used for wirework, but the serrated jaws can mark soft metals such as copper or aluminium.

Straightening a wire hanger

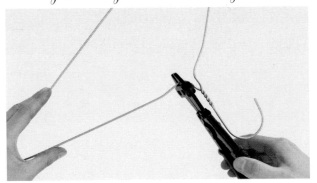

1 Cut the hanging loop and twisted section from the wire coat hanger using small bolt cutters.

2 Straighten the length you are left with – it may help to use locking pliers to straighten the corners.

Straightening wire

Pulling soft metal wire such as copper or aluminium to straighten it works well. Attach one end to a strong fixing point (a door handle for instance) and hold the other end in locking pliers. Pull until the wire is straight.

Binding wire together

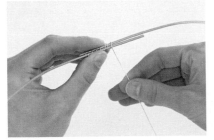

To bind two lengths of coat hanger wire together, overlap the ends by at least 5cm (2in) and wrap medium-gauge wire around the overlap until the ends are held firmly together.

Shaping wire

Gentle curves can be bent by hand, but for tighter curves in heavy-gauge wire, use a pair of ring-bending pliers – their smooth jaws do not mark the wire. If you're following a template, have it nearby for reference.

Twisting wires

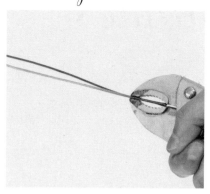

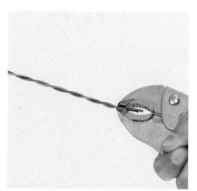

1 If you need a long length of twisted wire, bend a length of wire in half, attach it to a strong fixing point (a door handle works well) and lock the two ends in a pair of locking pliers.

2 Pull the wire taut and turn the locking pliers until you have an even twist along the whole length. Cut the wire to remove it from the fixing point.

Joining wires

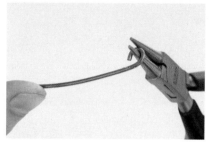

If you're working with wire and it breaks or runs out, attach another length by making a tiny loop in the end of each wire using round-nose pliers. Link the loops together, and press them closed with locking pliers.

Wrapping wire

Cut a length of medium-gauge wire one and a half times the length of the main wire. Curl the end of the medium wire around one end of the main wire, then wrap it around. Maintain tension so it is wrapped tightly and spaced evenly.

Making a circular base

Bend a length of wire to form a circle. Overlap the ends by 4cm (1½in). Wrap a short length of medium-gauge wire around the overlap to hold the structure together.

Making a hanging jar

1 Cut a length of medium-gauge wire about 55cm (21½in) long and wrap it once around the jar, just below the lip. Twist the end around the wire to secure.

2 Pull the free end of the wire over to form a handle, then thread it under the loop around the jar. Twist to secure it onto the ring. Trim any excess wire.

Making an "S" hook

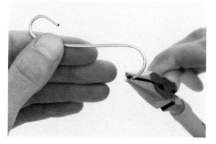

To make an S-shaped hook, curl one end of a 10cm (4in) piece of coat hanger wire outwards using pliers. Curve the other end inwards to create a small loop.

Wire heart decoration

This simple, decorative wire heart makes a perfect gift for a close friend. It's fashioned from a wire coat hanger and a handful of mother-of-pearl buttons. If you can't find any suitable buttons, use beads instead.

Materials

- Wire coat hanger
- Fine 0.4mm silver-plated wire
- Mother-of-pearl buttons

Equipment

- Small bolt cutters
- Ring-bending pliers
- Wire cutters
- Superglue

1 Cut the hanging loop off the hanger and straighten the hanger. Bend it into a heart shape, using your hands and ring-bending pliers. Cut a 2.5m (8ft 2in) length of fine wire with wire cutters. At the top of the heart, where the curves meet, join the ends of the coat hanger wire with four or five turns of fine wire. Pull the wire tight, leaving a 5cm (2in) tail. Add a drop of superglue to fix the wire in position and leave to dry.

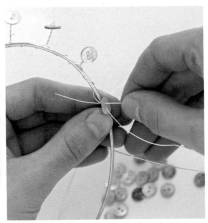

2 With the long end of the fine wire, make two loose turns along about 2cm (¾in) of the heart, then pull the end of the wire up through one hole in a button and back down through the other hole. Take care not to kink the wire as you pull it through.

3 Hold the button 1.5cm (⅝in) from the heart and grip the two pieces of fine wire where they meet the heart. Rotate the button to twist the wire. Make two more turns of the fine wire around the heart, add another button, then repeat all the way round.

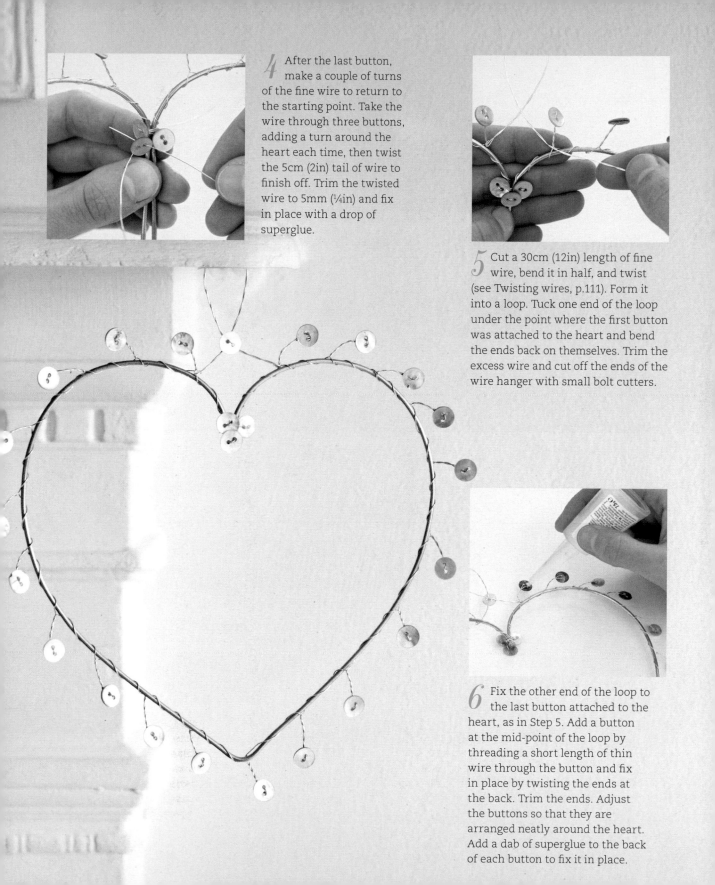

4 After the last button, make a couple of turns of the fine wire to return to the starting point. Take the wire through three buttons, adding a turn around the heart each time, then twist the 5cm (2in) tail of wire to finish off. Trim the twisted wire to 5mm (¼in) and fix in place with a drop of superglue.

5 Cut a 30cm (12in) length of fine wire, bend it in half, and twist (see Twisting wires, p.111). Form it into a loop. Tuck one end of the loop under the point where the first button was attached to the heart and bend the ends back on themselves. Trim the excess wire and cut off the ends of the wire hanger with small bolt cutters.

6 Fix the other end of the loop to the last button attached to the heart, as in Step 5. Add a button at the mid-point of the loop by threading a short length of thin wire through the button and fix in place by twisting the ends at the back. Trim the ends. Adjust the buttons so that they are arranged neatly around the heart. Add a dab of superglue to the back of each button to fix it in place.

Wire chandelier

It's amazing to think that a few wire coat hangers and glass jars can be transformed into something so spectacular! Wrapped wire hangers form a stable structure for this chandelier, and the curled ends add a touch of elegance. Recycle small glass yogurt or babyfood jars and fill them with tealights to create hanging lanterns.

Materials

- 10 wire coat hangers
- Small bolt cutters
- Medium-gauge wire
- Wire cutters
- Long-nose pliers
- 8 small glass yogurt or babyfood jars with a lip
- 8 tealights
- Wire or ribbon

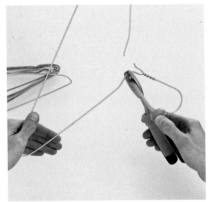

1 Cut off the hanging loops and straighten all 10 hangers (see Straightening a wire hanger, p.110). Cut lengths of medium-gauge wire one-and-a-half times longer than the length of the straightened hangers. Wrap this wire evenly around nine of the hanger wires. These will be used to construct the frame of the chandelier, while the plain wire will be cut into lengths and used to hang the jars.

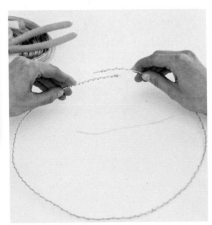

2 Use one of the wrapped wires to make a circle 27.5cm (11in) in diameter. This is the top tier. Overlap the ends of the wire and wrap a short length of wire around the overlap to secure.

3 Make the bottom tier by joining two lengths of wrapped wire together to make one long length, overlapping the ends by 12.5cm (5in). Wrap the overlap with a short length of wire. Bend the wire into a circle 36cm (14in) in diameter and secure the ends.

4 To make the hanging device, shape the ends of two lengths of wrapped wire into decorative curls, as shown. Wrap the other ends at opposite sides of the top tier using long-nose pliers. Cover the joins where they meet the tier by wrapping with wire. Wrap a short length of wire just below the two curls and again a little farther down to keep the two wrapped wires together.

5 To attach the pillars that link the tiers, curl a wrapped wire around the top tier using long-nose pliers, then wrap the other end around the bottom tier, 30cm (12in) along its length. Shape the end of the wire to create a curl. Wire-wrap the joins on both tiers and repeat to make the three other pillars, spacing them out evenly.

6 Make eight hanging jars (see Making a hanging jar, p.111). Suspend the jars from "S" hooks made from 4in (10cm) lengths of the remaining non-wrapped wire. Drop a tealight in each jar and hang four jars on each tier. Finally, tie a wire or ribbon through the central stem at the top of the chandelier to hang it.

Mosaic bowl

This calming, woodland-inspired mosaic bowl is created using the direct method, meaning that tiles are glued straight onto the object and then grouted. This will not produce a completely level surface, resulting in a tactile bowl.

1 Draw a wavy line onto your bowl, about 4.5cm (1¾in) from the rim. Draw a second line 1.5cm (⅝in) below this one. This will be the first accent line on your bowl.

2 Prepare your tiles by soaking or peeling off any backing sheets. Select the plain tiles and those for the accent lines, and place them in groups of the same colour and type.

3 Cut tiles for the accent lines. Wearing goggles, hold the tile between thumb and forefinger and, positioning nippers at the edge, gently squeeze. Repeat to cut into quarters.

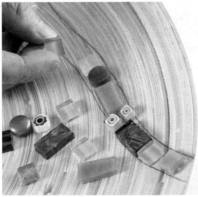

4 Arrange the tiles and embellishments between your wavy lines. Vary iridescent and matte tiles, as well as round and rectangular ones, to create a pattern.

Materials

- Wooden bowl
- Tesserae in different shades of green
- Flat-backed beads and 5mm (¼in) millefiori beads
- PVA glue
- Mosaic grout (either premixed or made according to the manufacturer's instructions)

Equipment

- Pencil
- Tile nippers
- Rubber gloves
- Protective mask & goggles
- Grout spreader
- Sponge
- Lint-free cloth

5 Move the pieces off the line, keeping their order. Add a dab of glue to the back of each piece and stick each one to your bowl, leaving even gaps in between.

6 For the lines of plain tiles, start with the lightest green tiles and cut them in half (see Step 3). Glue them on each side of the accent line, trimming them if necessary.

7 Complete one line at a time, increasing or decreasing the shade and adding accent lines at regular intervals. When complete, let the bowl dry overnight.

8 Wearing rubber gloves and a mask, apply the grout generously to the mosaic, working in different directions. Make sure to grout around the outer edge of the bowl, too.

9 Using a damp sponge, carefully wipe away the excess grout. Let dry for 20 minutes, then, before the grout is hard, wipe gently again.

10 When the grout is completely dry, use a lint-free dry cloth to wipe away any residue and polish the tiles to a shine.

Mosaic variations

Flower garland mirror

You will need

- Mirror with wide, flat, wooden frame
- A selection of tiles and glass pebbles
- White grout

Make this mirror in the same way as the mosaic bowl on pp.116–19. Draw on a floral design of your choice first and seal the wooden frame with watered-down PVA glue if necessary. Create the flowers first, starting with a glass pebble and using tile nippers to shape the petals. Make the leaf garlands in the same manner. Fill in the gaps around the designs with randomly cut tiles – a technique known as "crazy paving". Use tile halves to fill in the outer edge of the border. Cover the mirror with masking tape to protect it when grouting. Grout the frame, making sure to create a straight edge around the mirror.

Owl jewellery box

You will need

- Wooden box
- Glazed and unglazed ceramic tiles
- Glass nuggets and beads
- White grout
- Felt for base

This pretty jewellery box is made using the same technique as the mosaic bowl on pp.116–19. Start by drawing an owl design on the top of the box and then seal the box with watered-down PVA glue. Start filling in the design, attaching the nuggets and whole tiles first. Cut the remaining tiles to size to complete the design. Finally, fill in the area around the design with crazy paving (see Flower garland mirror method, left). Allow to dry and then grout the lid. Grout the box one side at a time, waiting for each side to dry before starting the next. Glue felt to the base to finish the box.

Round tealight holder

You will need

• Ball-shaped, wooden tealight holder

• Old crockery, broken into small pieces

• Tiles and glass pebbles

• White grout

• Felt for the bottom

This tealight holder is made in the same way as the mosaic bowl (see pp.116–19), but using fragments of broken crockery. First, draw a design of your choice on the tealight holder and then seal it with watered-down PVA glue. Glue down the glass pebbles first, and then use tile nippers to shape the crockery pieces into petals. Next, add any whole tiles. Finally, fill in the area around the design with more crockery pieces. Work a small area at a time. Some tiles may have to be held in place using tape until they dry. Grout, allow to dry, and attach felt to the bottom to finish.

Seaside coasters

You will need

• MDF squares

• Tiles in a variety of colours

• Grey grout

These seaside-inspired coasters have been made out of squares of MDF, using the technique described for the mosaic bowl on pp.116–19. Using your own design, first draw guidelines onto the coaster in pencil. Fill in the design first, shaping the tiles to fit. Try to keep the tiles fairly flat, since you will need to be able to rest a glass or mug on the coaster when finished. Next, fill in the background using square tiles, shaping them to fit as necessary. Again, try to keep the tiles as flat as possible. Grout the coasters, not forgetting the edges, to finish.

Fabric notebook

A brightly coloured, cheery-looking notebook is always a welcome and useful gift, and if you have made it yourself it will be even more appreciated. An easy approach is to buy a ready-bound notebook and decorate the cover, but stitching and binding the paper folios together and then covering them is quite straightforward once you get the hang of it.

1 Align the 12 folios, with folds on the same side. Pierce six evenly spaced holes in each folio with a pin, then sew the folios together with running stitch.

2 Cut the piece of muslin cloth so that it is the same length and width as the joined folios. Glue it over the stitched folio folds to make a spine.

3 Glue the rectangles (the thinnest in the middle) to the fabric with a slight gap between. Glue down the fabric edges. Glue the page half over the cover.

4 Glue half of each folded paper to an inside cover. Stick the spine to the cover, then glue the other half of each paper to an outer folio page.

Materials

- Approximately 60 sheets of A4 paper divided into 12 piles of 5 sheets of paper: each pile is then folded in half to make a "folio"

- Strip of muslin cloth

- 2 rectangles of recycled cardboard cut to the same size as the folios, and another thin strip for the spine

- Old, pretty recycled fabric cut just slightly larger than a sheet of paper

- 1 illustrated page from an old, unwanted book

- 2 sheets of brightly coloured recycled A4 paper, folded in half

Equipment

- Pin

- Linen thread and darning needle

- Eco-friendly adhesive glue

Decorated photo album

Although this decorated cover will always be delicate, it turns an ordinary-looking album into a beautiful, personalized gift. Choose a photo album or a large notebook with a neutral cloth or cardboard cover and good-quality, thick paper. Gather leaves as they start to turn rich, autumnal colours and look for interesting seed heads, grasses, and other natural materials.

Materials

- 1 photo album
- Variety of natural materials dried flat (p.12)
- Eco-friendly adhesive glue

Tip

Save tissue paper

Reserve any sheets of tissue paper that are wrapped around goods you buy or receive and, using an iron on a low setting, iron out the creases. Use the tissue paper to cover and protect delicate items like this album cover when not in use.

1 When your natural materials are all flattened and thoroughly dried, glue a row of seed heads or leaves along the top of the front cover.

2 For each subsequent row, glue on materials that are roughly the same size in a pattern. Overlap or alternate some materials.

3 Continue to build up the pattern by glueing on rows of coloured leaves, grasses, and twigs until the front cover is completely filled up.

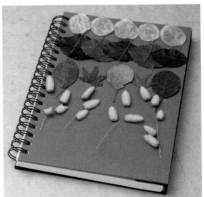

4 Leave the glued materials to dry, then cover the book carefully in several layers of tissue paper before gift-wrapping it in a recycled box.

Hot-water bottle cover

This lovely winter gift is quite simple to make and will delight anyone who receives it. Collect scraps of pretty cotton material or look in secondhand or charity shops for natural fabrics with vintage patterns and colours to make the details on this cover really unique. If you don't have an old blanket to use for the cover, use any thick, recycled soft fabric.

Materials

- Template (p.245–47)
- Woollen blanket or similar thick material
- Decorative shapes, such as stars, hearts, or strips, cut from scraps of fabric
- 2 recycled or vintage buttons

Equipment

- Scissors
- Pins
- Cotton thread and needle or sewing machine
- Coloured embroidery thread and needle for blanket stitch

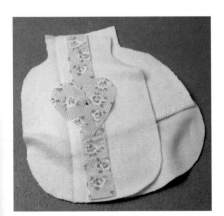

1 Using the template, cut a front panel, two back half-panels, and two matching decorative shapes. Pin the shapes to the front of the cover.

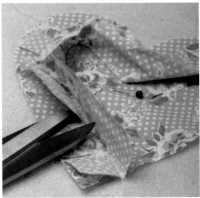

2 Sew the fabric shapes onto the front panel, leaving a seam 1cm (½in) wide. Snip the fabric edges every 1cm (½in) to make a ruffle.

3 Sew the buttons onto the fabric shape. Sew the panels together, leaving a seam of 6mm (¼in). The back panels should overlap slightly.

4 Using the coloured embroidery thread and needle, sew all the way around the edges of the cover using blanket stitch.

Savoury Christmas hamper

A decorated wicker basket filled with homemade chutney (pp.174–75), a bag of sweet chestnuts (pp.164–65), pickled shallots (pp.170–71), and flavoured oil (pp.178–83), makes a delightful gift.

Sweet Christmas hamper

Give a variety of sweet, homemade produce as a gift: package up chocolate brownies (pp.196–97), mini panettone (pp.192–93), and cranberry jelly (pp.176–77) in pretty boxes and decorated jars, and arrange them in a hamper.

Natural Christmas cards

If you want to post any of these homemade three-dimensional cards, choose those with the least delicate, flattest decorations and cut a piece of recycled card the same size as the card. Cover the front of the decorated card with the card before sealing it in an envelope. This should, hopefully, protect the decorations from disintegrating or breaking in transit.

1 Cut a piece of recycled card to the correct size. Score lightly down the middle of the card in a straight line using a scalpel and ruler.

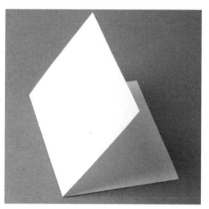

2 Fold the card in half along the scored line, which will ensure a clean fold down the centre of the card.

3 Arrange and stick a dried leaf onto the front of the card using small dabs of glue.

4 Glue two smaller leaves onto the larger leaf and attach one star anise at the base of the leaves. Then leave to one side to dry completely.

Materials

- Recycled card
- Found objects such as seedheads, twigs, and leaves in different sizes, dried flat (p.12)
- Spices such as star anise and cinnamon sticks
- Dried ingredients such as orange slices and bay leaves

Equipment

- Scissors
- Scalpel
- Ruler
- Eco-friendly adhesive glue

Recycled paper cards

These cards are easy to make, and are a fun, child-friendly project. Tear out pages from old magazines with interesting patterns, illustrations, and festive photographs, or recycle wrapping paper, wallpaper samples, or the pictures from last year's Christmas cards. Use a selection of templates from the back of the book to cut out different shapes, or download some from the internet.

Materials

- Template (pp.240–43)
- Recycled pictures
- Plain, recycled card (or find ready-made, plain recycled cards)

Equipment

- Scissors
- Scalpel
- Ruler
- Eco-friendly adhesive glue

Tip

Recycle your old cards
Converting timber into paper is a very energy-intensive process. If all Christmas cards sent in the UK were recycled, around 250,000 trees would be saved.

1 Draw a template of your choice and cut it out. If you are using the star template, make up the small star template as well.

2 Place the template on a piece of illustrated or patterned recycled paper. Draw around the template and cut out the shape.

3 Lightly score down the middle of the recycled card with a scalpel and ruler. Fold the card in half and glue the star shape onto the front.

4 Using the smallest star template, cut tiny stars from the recycled paper and glue them onto the card around the main star. Allow to dry.

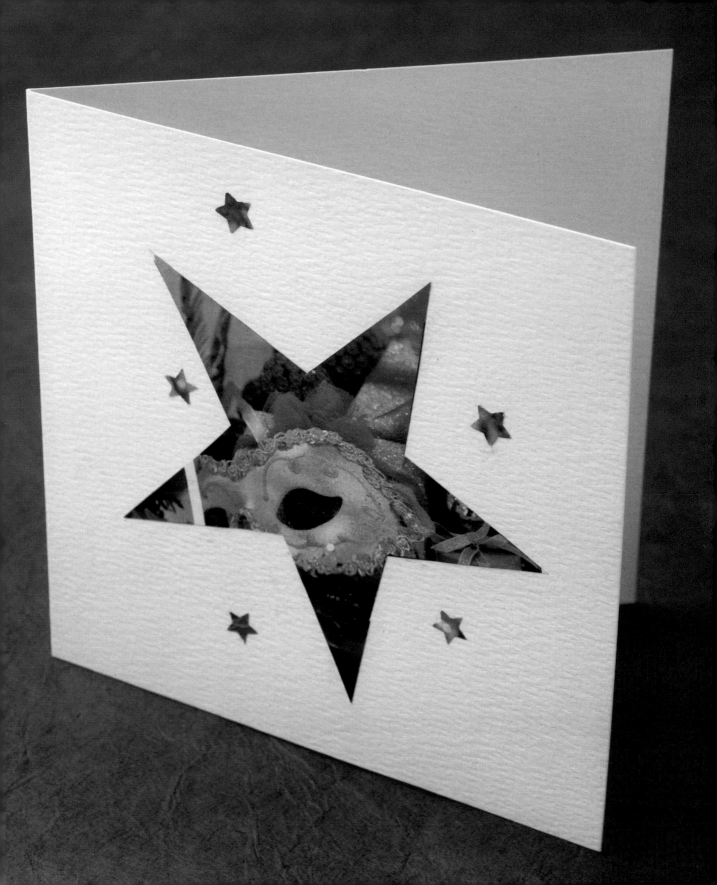

Fabric Christmas cards

These attractive cards can be easily adapted: use a loop of ribbon instead of string, or punch two small holes close together near the top of the card, thread through wool or twine, and tie it in a bow; or cut out and sew together two fabric shapes and fill the centre with sweet-smelling dried lavender. Don't cut the shapes too small, or the edges may fray.

1 Make up your chosen template, then place it on a piece of fabric and cut around the shape neatly with a pair of scissors.

2 Thread the string through the button or bead and secure the ends of the string in a knot.

3 Glue the knotted end of the string loop onto the back of the fabric shape and allow to dry.

4 Lightly score down the middle of the card with a scalpel and ruler. Glue the fabric shape onto the front of the card. Allow to dry.

Materials

- Template (pp.240–43)
- Scraps of fabric, or old carpet samples, for an interesting texture
- Recycled string
- Recycled or vintage buttons or beads
- Recycled card

Equipment

- Scissors
- Eco-friendly adhesive glue
- Scalpel
- Ruler

Jewellery case

This slim case makes the perfect gift box for jewellery and other small items likely to slip out of a looser box. Wrap your gift in tissue paper and close the box with a ribbon tied in a bow to ensure that it stays safe until opened.

1 Use a photocopier to resize the template, if necessary. Transfer it onto a sheet of card using tracing paper and a pencil.

2 Flip the card over. Glue a sheet of tissue paper or decorative paper to the card, making sure that it is stuck down completely. You can also use patterned card.

3 Using a scalpel and a cutting mat, cut around the outside lines of the box. Make sure not to cut into the folding lines.

4 Using a ruler and one side of a pair of scissors, or a blunt knife, score along all the internal folding lines. Erase the pencil lines.

Materials
- Template (p.250)
- Card
- Tracing paper
- Tissue paper

Equipment
- Glue stick
- Pencil
- Scalpel
- Cutting mat
- Ruler
- Pair of scissors or blunt knife
- Eraser

5 Fold the side flap up and spread glue on the patterned side. Fold the case in half and attach the flap to the inside of the opposite edge. Hold it in place until it sticks.

6 Choose one end to be the bottom of the case. Fold in the first flap along the curved line, and then the other. Fill the box and fold in the flaps at the other end to close.

Pyramid boxes
(see overleaf)

Pyramid boxes

These small boxes are quick and easy to make and require no glue.
They are the ideal size for a small gift, or to hold sweets or party favours.
Personalize your boxes by using different colours and types of ribbon.

Materials

- Template (p.251)
- Patterned card, or patterned paper glued onto card (see p.143)
- Tracing paper
- Ribbon

Equipment

- Pencil
- Scalpel
- Cutting mat
- Blunt knife (or pair of scissors)
- Eraser
- Hole punch

1 Use a photocopier to resize the template, if necessary. Transfer it onto a sheet of patterned card using tracing paper and a pencil.

2 Using a scalpel and a cutting mat, cut around the outside of the box template. Make sure not to cut into the internal folding lines.

3 Lightly score along the fold lines using a ruler and a blunt knife (or one side of a pair of scissors).

4 Add a hole to the tip of each triangle using a hole punch. Try to keep them evenly spaced and make sure they are not too close to the edges in any direction.

5 For a neat finish, erase the fold lines. Fold each section and flap along the scored lines, making sure that each crease is sharp.

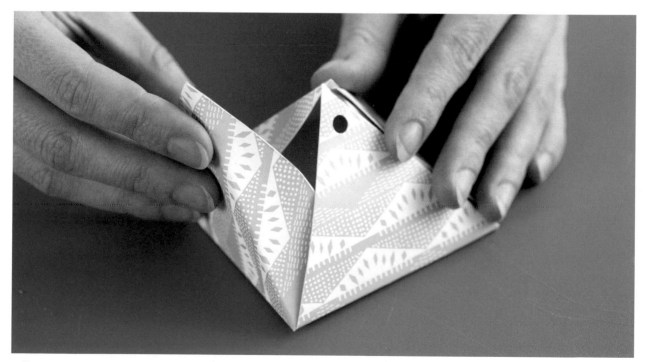

6 Assemble the pyramid box by folding in each side and tucking each flap into the centre of the box. Fasten the box by threading a ribbon through the holes and tying a knot or bow.

Square gift box

A gift box is the ideal way to present awkwardly shaped gifts. You can make this gift box exactly the required size by resizing the template. Use patterned card, or glue decorative paper to card before you create different looks.

Materials

- Template (p.249)
- Patterned card, or patterned paper glued onto card (see p.143)
- Tracing paper

Equipment

- Pencil
- Scalpel
- Cutting mat
- Ruler
- Blunt knife (or pair of scissors)
- Eraser
- Glue stick
- Tissue paper (optional)

1 Use a photocopier to resize the template, if necessary. Transfer it onto a sheet of patterned card using tracing paper and a pencil.

2 Using a scalpel and a cutting mat, cut around the outside of the box template. Make sure not to cut into the internal folding lines.

3 Once you have cut out the entire shape, score all the folding lines using a ruler and blunt knife, or one side of a pair of scissors. This will make the box easier to assemble.

4 Fold the sides inwards along the scored lines, making sure that each crease is sharp. For a neat finish, erase the pencil lines along the creases inside the box.

5 Attach the three sides not adjacent to the lid to each other using the glue stick or double-sided tape on the outside of the flaps. Hold in place until set.

6 Fold in the flaps of the last remaining side, spread glue or attach tape to the patterned side of the flaps, and slot the side into place. Press the flaps down and hold in place until set.

7 Line the box with tissue paper, if required, and place your chosen gift inside. Close the lid, sealing the flap with glue or tape if necessary. The boxes can be left plain, or decorated with ribbon or paper (see pp.150–51).

Decorating gift boxes

A few odds and ends (coloured paper, ribbons, tissue paper, and buttons) can turn plain wrapped packages or dull boxes into beautiful, personalized gifts.

Gift tag and ribbon

Cut a luggage-label shape from white card. Punch a hole in the corner and thread through with ribbon. Tie this ribbon around the box and glue the ends at the base of the box. Tie another ribbon in a different colour around the box.

Button bow

Cut out four rectangles in two colours of patterned card. Cut a triangle out of one end of each. Glue to the top of the box, layered on top of one another. Cut out a bow-tie shape from patterned card. Fold the sides of the bow-tie shape around and under to meet at the back. Glue this to the box and press down to make the bow shape. Glue a button to the centre of the bow.

Floral wrap

Wrap a length of ribbon around the box and glue at the bottom. Add another ribbon going the other way. Cut out flower shapes in different colours from tissue paper and layer on top of each other. Sew a few stitches to hold the flowers together. Glue the flowers on the box where the ribbons meet. Add a few extra smaller flowers, using the same method.

Lots of dots

Layer sheets of tissue paper in different colours. Cut circles out of the sheets of tissue paper, cutting through all the layers. Using a needle and thread, sew a few small stitches through the centre of each stack of circles to secure them and tie off at the back. Glue these to the box top.

Button band

Cut out a strip of patterned card long enough to wrap around the box. Sew on a variety of buttons using cream embroidery thread or yarn. Wrap the strip around the box and glue at the bottom.

Rosette

Cut two lengths of ribbon and point the ends by cutting out a triangle. Glue these to the top of the box. Using pinking shears, cut circles from patterned card and decorative papers. Cut each circle smaller as you go and stack them up to make the rosette shape. Thread a button through the circles to hold them together, then glue them on the box.

Recycled gift wrapping

Part of the pleasure of being given an imaginatively wrapped, beautifully presented gift is guessing just what might be underneath all the wrapping. If your gift is an unusual shape, put it in a discarded box first and then take the trouble to wrap the gift carefully, so that the recycled materials you choose will look their best.

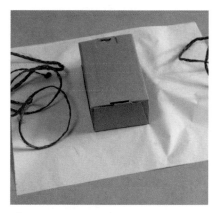

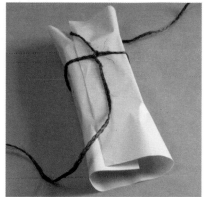

1 Put the gift in the box; shapes with flat, angular sides are easier to wrap neatly. Place the box in the centre of the paper.

2 Fold two sides of the paper over the box so they overlap. Wrap the string around the box and tie it in a knot to hold the folded paper in place.

3 Fold the paper carefully at each end of the box: press the paper neatly in towards the centre to create two triangular flaps at either end.

4 Fold down the flaps so they overlap. Wrap the string over the flaps to hold them in place, turn the box over, and secure the string in a bow.

Materials

- Recycled cardboard box large enough to hold the gift (optional)

- Clean sheet of recycled paper, ironed on a low setting to get rid of creases

- Coloured string or ribbon (iron the ribbon on a low setting, or run through heated hair straighteners, to get rid of any creases)

Tip

Avoid using sticky tape
Paper can't be reused if it is covered in tape, so use ribbon, twine, upholstery trimmings, raffia, wool, or string instead. Use paper-based, water-activated gummed tape to mail a gift; PVC tape has a negative impact on the environment.

Gift wrapping variations

Tea towel and vintage tartan ribbon Use a colourful tea towel and ribbon – the tea towel could even form part of the gift.

Brown paper and woven string Use recycled brown paper and make an attractive ribbon by weaving together lengths of string.

Newspaper and garden string Sheets of newspaper are a simple option, but look stylish. Tie with green string for a festive look.

Tissue paper and leaves Arrange leaves between sheets of recycled tissue paper. Secure the wrapping with glue and string.

Printed paper Tear pages from an old atlas, a map of a well-loved area, or a colour magazine to make this unusual wrapping.

Paper and corrugated cardboard Over-wrap recycled paper with ridged cardboard for textural interest. Secure with a ribbon.

Vintage fabric and string Use trimmed oddments of beautiful fabric to wrap gifts. Tie simply with festively coloured string.

Recycled shirt Cut the back off an old shirt and wrap the shirt front around the gift. Secure the sleeves on top with string.

Decorate gifts

Sometimes the smallest touches make all the difference, and a pile of packages under the tree can look so much more enticing if they are thoughtfully decorated. Be creative by choosing natural and recycled everyday items and trimmings instead of the usual ready-made, bought alternatives to make your wrapped gifts look special.

Create a gift hamper

A recycled basket, or one made of willow or wicker from sustainable sources, makes an ideal hamper (see pp.128–31).

Line the hamper with plenty of natural material like hay or straw.

Decorate jars and bottles of home-made produce with vintage fabric and ribbon.

Fill small linen sacks with nuts, fresh herbs, or biscuits.

Arrange the produce on the hay so that all the labels are clearly visible.

Cut a few lengths of holly or mistletoe and tuck them inside the rim of the basket around the gifts.

Recycled and vintage items

Save brightly coloured ribbon from your own gifts and purchases, or look out for vintage ribbon, iron it with a cool iron or pull it through a pair of heated hair straighteners, and tie it around gifts wrapped in brown paper. If you have a few old beads and buttons, sew or glue them onto the ribbon to create a charming, detailed effect, or thread them onto string or twine and secure the ends in a knot.

Natural raffia

Raffia is made from mulberry tree bark, which regenerates, so no trees are cut down to produce it. Gather a few lengths of raffia together, or plait them, wrap them around a gift, and tie them in an extravagant bow.

Found materials

Collect attractive natural materials and fresh foliage: pine cones, holly leaves, trailing ivy, sprigs of bright berries, dried leaves (p.12), sliced dried fruit (p.64), and cinnamon sticks all make lovely and unique final touches when tied on top of gifts.

Gift tags

Cut festive motifs from recycled patterned paper, felt, or fabric and stick or sew them onto luggage labels or small pieces of card to make gift tags; they will look much more striking than bought labels. Alternatively, stick on dried star anise and cardamom pods in simple patterns for delightfully aromatic gift tags.

Decorated gift variations

Cinnamon sticks and braided raffia Tie the gift with plaited raffia, thread ribbon under it, and tie around cinnamon sticks.

Evergreen foliage and string Gather a few lengths of string, tie up the gift, and tuck a couple of sprigs of foliage under the bow.

Pine cones and raffia Tie the gift with raffia, wrap a little thin wire around the base of each cone, and tie them to the bow.

Dried fruits and raffia Glue three dried orange slices together in an overlapped row, tie the gift with raffia, and glue on the slices.

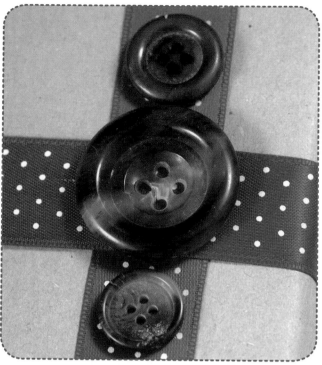

Raffia and dried leaves Gather a few lengths of raffia, tie the gift, and glue on a few dried, flattened leaves just under the bow.

Ribbons and buttons Wrap recycled ribbon around the gift and glue different-sized buttons onto the ribbon.

Holly sprig and vintage ribbon Tie the gift with bright vintage ribbon and tuck a holly sprig with a few berries under the bow.

Threaded buttons Thread odd buttons onto a very thin length of ribbon and tie the ribbon around the gift.

Gift label variations

Dried leaf star label Glue a dried, flattened leaf (p.12) onto recycled card, cut a star shape, and glue a nut in the centre.

Fabric star label Glue some cheery fabric onto recycled card, cut into a star shape, and glue on a dried bay leaf and old button.

Mini star gift tag Cut out a fabric star, glue it onto folded recycled card, and decorate with a button and a little raffia loop.

Rustic bead label Push both ends of a length of garden string through a hole, thread beads onto each end, and tie in a knot.

Skeleton leaf label Thread a piece of string through the hole of a label and glue a couple of dried, flattened leaves over the hole.

Paper dove label Cut a dove template from recycled cardboard, glue on festive-looking recycled paper, and cut it out.

Paper holly leaf label Cut a holly leaf shape out of recycled paper, glue onto recycled card, and add a button.

Fresh holly leaf label Sew a holly leaf onto a luggage label with festive-coloured embroidery thread using simple running stitch.

Homemade
Edible Treats

Roasting chestnuts

To roast a handful of chestnuts over an open fire, choose a cast-iron pan, or buy a special roasting pan that has holes punched into the base. Use a sharp knife to make a small incision at the tip of each nut, and roast over a medium flame for about 15 minutes.

Spiced nuts

These coated nuts make a crunchy, moreish homemade snack that is a tasty change from ordinary nuts and crisps. If you prefer, you can substitute the spices for either cumin seeds, sesame seeds, nigella seeds, or a few chilli flakes. Store any leftover nuts in an airtight jar and eat them within three days.

1 If you have bought unshelled nuts, remove all the shells. Finely chop the rosemary leaves, and discard the tough stalks.

2 Melt the butter and sugar in a large, heavy saucepan or frying pan on a low heat. Add the chopped rosemary, cayenne pepper, paprika, and salt and then toss in the nuts.

3 Stir until the nuts are evenly coated with the spice mix. Toast on a low heat, stirring or tossing frequently until the coated nuts look golden brown and crisp.

4 Tip the nuts onto a large sheet of greaseproof paper, arrange in a single layer, and leave to cool before placing in small bowls. Serve alongside root crisps (pp.168–69).

Ingredients

Serves 6–8

- 300g (10½oz) mixed unsalted nuts
- A few sprigs of fresh rosemary
- 30g (1½oz) unsalted butter
- 2 tbsp soft dark brown sugar
- ½ tsp cayenne pepper
- 2 tsp mild Spanish paprika
- A good pinch of sea salt

Oven-dried root and fruit crisps

These are very pretty, and you can use them as a party snack or garnish. For an extra kick, try sprinkling them with smoked sweet paprika.

1 Preheat oven to 180°C (350°F).

2 Use either the slicing attachment on a food processor, a mandoline, or a Japanese vegetable slicer to slice the unpeeled sweet potato, beetroot, parsnip, apple, and pear ⅓cm (⅛in) thick. Place the slices in a single layer on oiled baking trays. Put into the oven.

3 Reduce oven temperature to 120°C (250°F). Bake for 1½ hours, turning the slices over every 20 minutes, until dried. Cool in single layers on wire racks. Sprinkle with salt. Serve at room temperature, with or without dips.

Get ahead
Make up to 1 day in advance. Store in an airtight container at room temperature.

Ingredients

Makes about 150g (5½oz)

- 1 small sweet potato, unpeeled
- 1 small beetroot, unpeeled
- 1 small parsnip, unpeeled
- 1 apple, unpeeled
- 1 pear, unpeeled
- 2 tsp salt

Equipment

- Either a food processor with a slicing attachment, a mandoline, or a Japanese vegetable slicer

Pickled vegetables

If you have an abundance of fresh vegetables, pickle some of them in homemade spiced pickling vinegar to preserve them for the Christmas season, or to give away in a gift hamper. The pickling process transforms the taste and texture of these fresh vegetables into more complex flavours, which taste good with a variety of different foods such as fish, game, and cold meats.

Homemade spiced pickling vinegar

Ingredients

- 1¼ litres (2 pints) malt vinegar
- A few pieces of blade mace
- 20 cloves
- 20 whole allspice berries
- 1 cinnamon stick
- 6 peppercorns
- 225g (8oz) demerara sugar

1. Boil all the ingredients together in a pan for a few minutes. Then cover and leave the liquid for 2 hours to cool completely. Strain into sterilized bottles until needed.

2. Use preserving jars with vinegar-proof lids when you bottle the vegetables in pickling vinegar. Leave the pickles to mature for at least three months before using them.

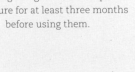

Salt, oil, and vinegar all prevent vegetables from decay by protecting them from the bacteria that could rot them. Salt draws out moisture and creates an inhospitable environment for bacteria, oil coats the produce to prevent contamination from the air, and the acid in vinegar, known as acetic acid, inhibits bacterial growth. Pickling combines the preservative qualities of salt and vinegar, and it's an ideal way to preserve vegetables such as beans, cabbage, cauliflower, cucumbers, onions, and shallots. Use the freshest, crispest produce for the best results.

Brining and potting up

The vegetables need "brining" in salt water first before being preserved in vinegar, to draw out the moisture that would otherwise seep into the vinegar and dilute it. The brining time varies: dense vegetables such as shallots need longer than beans or cucumbers. Use coarse salt, as it contains none of the anti-caking agents that are added to table salt. For 1.5kg (3¼lb) of shallots, mix 4.5 litres (8 pints) of water and 450g (1lb) salt into a brine, add the shallots, and leave for 12 hours with a plate on top to weigh the shallots down and keep them submerged. Then skin the shallots and cover them with fresh brine for a further 24 hours before placing them in sterilized preserving jars. Pour over the spiced pickling vinegar (see left) to completely cover them, and then seal the jars. As well as preserving the vegetables, this spiced pickling vinegar adds a lovely delicate flavour.

Preserved lemons

If lemons are salted and left to cure in a jar, the rind turns into a rich, rounded flavour that adds a marvellously distinctive Middle-Eastern flavour to dishes. Chop the rind and rub it with garlic over a chicken or leg of lamb before roasting, mix it with roasted onions, garlic, and pumpkin pieces, some cooked couscous, raisins, pine nuts, and a stick of cinnamon, or add it to slow-cooked casserole dishes.

Ingredients

These quantities are approximate, but should fill a 1-litre (1¾-pint) jar; adjust the quantities accordingly.

- 5 unwaxed organic lemons
- 500g (1lb 1½oz) coarse sea salt
- 2 cinnamon sticks (optional)
- 1 tbsp coriander seeds (optional)
- 1 tbsp whole cumin seeds (optional)
- 1 tsp black peppercorns
- 1 tsp cloves (optional)
- 3 dried red chillies (optional)
- Dried bay leaves
- Enough freshly squeezed lemon juice to cover the contents of the jar

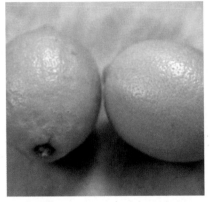

1 Sterilize the preserving jar. Wipe the lemons to remove any dirt.

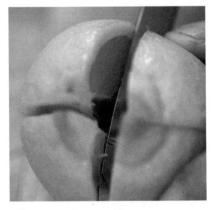

2 Cut two thirds of the way through each lemon with a sharp knife, then again at right angles to the first cut.

3 Open out the top of each lemon slightly, fill the cuts with salt, and press the top of each lemon together again. Put a couple of lemons in the jar and pack the salt in around them.

4 Fill the jar with the salt, lemons, spices, and bay leaves. Cover with the lemon juice and seal. Leave for at least two months while the salt slowly dissolves to create a clear liquid.

Pear chutney

Use the largest heavy-based saucepan you have, or a preserving pan, to make chutney. As the ingredients simmer, check on them frequently and give them a stir so that they don't catch on the bottom of the pan and burn, which spoils the flavour. Then pot up the chutney in jars with vinegar-proof lids. To get a good spicy–sweet balance, leave the chutney to mature for at least three months.

1 Put all the fruit and vegetables in the pan with no added liquid and simmer gently, uncovered, until tender, stirring occasionally.

2 Wrap the peppercorns in the muslin. Tie with the string to make a sachet. Then add it and the remaining ingredients to the pan.

3 Simmer the chutney, uncovered, and stir often until it thickens and takes on a dark caramel colour. This will take two to three hours.

4 Remove the peppercorn sachet, pot up the chutney in warm, sterilized jars, and seal. Store the jars in a cool, dark place.

Ingredients

Makes about 2.5kg (6lb)

- 1.4kg (3lb) pears, peeled, cored and cut into 2cm (¾in) cubes
- 450g (1lb) onions, chopped
- 450g (1lb) green or red tomatoes, sliced
- 250g (8oz) raisins, chopped
- 6 peppercorns
- 700g (1½lb) brown sugar
- 1 tsp cayenne pepper
- 1 tsp ground ginger
- 2 tsp salt
- 750ml (1½ pints) malt vinegar

Equipment

- Small piece of muslin
- Length of string

Cranberry jelly

This tart, fruity preserve is not only perfect with a roast turkey or chicken on Christmas day, but it also complements pork, sausages, and any cold meats you may serve over the festive season. Store the jars in the larder or a cool, dark cabinet for up to one year. Once opened, a jar of jelly should keep well in the fridge for up to three weeks.

Ingredients

Makes about 500ml (1 pint) of jelly

- 450g (1lb) fresh cranberries
- 350ml (12fl oz) water
- 450g (1lb) caster sugar

Tip

Frozen cranberries

If you find it hard to find fresh cranberries, a bag of frozen fruits will work just as well for this recipe (avoid dried cranberries). There's no need to thaw the berries first before you cook them.

1 Check the cranberries and discard any that have brown spots or are shrivelled. Put the berries and water in a saucepan and bring to the boil over a medium heat.

2 Turn the heat down and simmer the mixture until the cranberries are tender. Then place a fine sieve over a bowl and pour the cranberry mixture into the sieve.

3 Press the berries through the sieve with a spoon to produce a smooth pulp in the bowl. Return the pulp and juice to the saucepan, bring to the boil, and add the sugar.

4 Allow the mix to simmer for 10 minutes, then test for the setting point. If the jelly sets when tested, pour into sterilized jars, seal, label, and date the jars.

Make flavoured oils

Homemade infused oils are a wonderfully instant way of adding an extra shot of flavour to your cooking. They make a perfect gift for food lovers and serious cooks alike, so bottle a selection of flavoured oils and add gift labels, or include one or two in a gift hamper. Try out the recipes on pp.180–83, or experiment with different flavourings, such as lemon peel, whole spices, or pink peppercorns.

Infused oils have the potential to support the growth of bacteria, so you should follow the procedures for bottling flavoured oils carefully, and make sure that any ingredients you use are washed and thoroughly dried first. Use pretty recycled bottles or jars for these oils.

Sterilizing equipment

It's important to sterilize all bottles or jars and their lids before adding any ingredients. Wash them in soapy water, or put them through a hot dishwasher wash, and leave to drain until nearly dry. Then place them upside down in a cold oven and heat them for 10–15 minutes at 150°C (300°F). Leave them upturned on a clean cloth until you are ready to use them so that dust or dirt, which could contaminate the product, can't be trapped inside. Alternatively, you can boil the bottles in a large saucepan covered with water for 15 minutes, dry them thoroughly with a fresh clean cloth, and upturn them onto another cloth until they are ready to be used.

Wash and thoroughly dry all ingredients to be used as flavourings before putting them in a bottle and adding the oil.

Making the oils

Make the flavoured oil a week before you need it. Put your choice of dry ingredients into a clear, sterilized glass bottle at least 1 litre (1¾ pints) in capacity, then carefully fill the bottle with light olive oil. Make sure the dry ingredients stay below the surface of the oil, or they may turn mouldy. Secure the lid firmly and shake well once a day for a week to allow the flavours to develop. Add a gift label with instructions to store the oil in the fridge.

Chilli oil

A bottle of chilli oil, packed with vibrant red chilli peppers, makes a beautiful and useful gift for any foodie in your life. It is also handy to have on standby for your own cooking: just few drops will add zing to any pizza or pasta dish.

1 Slice the regular chillies in half with a knife, cutting all the way through the stem. Add the sliced chillies, whole bird's eye chillies, and any seeds to the sterilized bottle.

Ingredients

- 1 litre (1¾ pints) light olive oil
- 100g (13½oz) mix of red bird's eye chillies and regular red chillies

Equipment

- Knife
- Cutting board
- Sterilized glass bottle with stopper
- Jug and funnel (optional)

2 Fill up the bottle with 1 litre (1¾ pints) olive oil and stopper it. The oil will keep for up to one month.

Flavoured oil variations

Basil oil

Fragrant basil oil makes a flavourful base for salad dressings, and it can be used to flavour sauces and soups. Bruising the leaves before you pour on the oil releases their delicate aroma.

Ingredients

- 1 litre (1¾ pints) light olive oil
- 150g (5oz) basil

1 Heat the oil gently in a pan until it reaches 40°C (104°F).

2 Lightly bruise the basil and put it in a warm, sterilized jar or bottle. Pour the warm oil into the jar, then seal. The oil will be ready to use in three to four weeks.

Garlic and rosemary oil

This traditionally flavoured oil can be used as a base for marinades, or to lightly coat vegetables before they are roasted in the oven. The oil keeps for one month.

Ingredients

- 6 garlic cloves
- 3 stalks rosemary
- 1 litre (1¾ pints) light olive oil

1 Crush the garlic cloves lightly. Place them in a sterilized jar or bottle with the stalks of rosemary.

2 Add oil to the bottle to cover the herbs, then seal.

Walnut bread

To help bread cook well, mist the inside of the oven with a water spray just before baking the dough. The loaf is baked if it sounds hollow when tapped on the base. This walnut bread will keep in a bread bin for up to four days, and it also freezes well. If you want to reheat it in a low oven, rub a little water over it beforehand to prevent it from drying out as it warms up.

Ingredients

Makes 2 ring loaves

- 400g (14oz) plain white bread flour
- 100g (3½oz) dark rye flour
- 1½ tsp dried yeast
- 2 tsp salt
- 320ml (12fl oz) tepid water
- 200g (7oz) walnuts, crushed

Tip

Kneading bread
The action of kneading warms and stretches the gluten in flour. This elasticity, and the action of yeast, gives bread its light, springy texture. Press and stretch the dough away from you, then lift the edges into the middle, give it a quarter turn, and repeat.

1 Preheat the oven to 230°C (450°F). Mix the flours together, then add the yeast and salt. Add a little tepid water and mix. Gradually add more water until the mixture becomes a dough.

2 Add the nuts to the dough, then knead the dough for 5–8 minutes until pliable. Place it in a lightly oiled bowl, cover with a damp tea towel, and leave it to rest until it doubles in size.

3 Turn the rested dough out onto a clean, lightly floured surface again and divide it into two equal amounts. Knead each half of the dough into a tight ball.

4 Shape each ball into a ring with a hole the size of a fist. Place on a lightly floured baking tray and cover with a damp tea towel until they double in size. Then bake for 20–25 minutes.

Focaccia bread

This bread tastes so good that it's unlikely you'll have much left over after serving it, but it keeps well in a bread safe for two days or so. When you turn the bread out onto a wire rack to cool after baking, drizzle a little olive oil over the surface. The bread will soak up the oil as it cools to give even more flavour.

1 Preheat the oven to 190°C (375°F). Roast the bulbs, cut side down, for 20 minutes or until soft. Squeeze cooked cloves from their skins. Mash lightly, leaving some cloves whole. Set aside.

2 Put the flour in a bowl and make a well in the centre. Add the yeast and salt, half the water, and all the oil. Using a fork, draw the flour from the edge of the bowl into the well.

3 Stir in the rest of the water, bit by bit, to form a dough. Knead the dough for 5 minutes, then leave it in a clean, lightly floured, covered bowl to rest for 1 hour. Knock out the air.

4 Spread out in a floured baking tray, rub in the olive oil, scatter over the garlic and rosemary, and rest, covered, for 30 minutes. Bake for 20 minutes or until the surface is golden brown.

Ingredients

- 3 whole garlic bulbs with their bases sliced off
- 500g (1lb 2oz) white self-raising flour
- 1 tsp fast-action dried yeast
- 1 tsp salt
- 300ml (½ pint) tepid water
- A good glug of olive oil – about 50ml (2fl oz)
- Fresh rosemary leaves, chopped, from several rosemary sprigs

Anadama bread

This dark, sweet cornbread originally hails from New England. It is curiously sweet and savoury at the same time. Serve with Emmental or Gruyère cheese, or buttered and topped with ham and mustard.

Ingredients

- 120ml (4fl oz) whole milk
- 750g (1lb 10oz) polenta or fine yellow cornmeal
- 50g (1¾oz) unsalted butter, softened
- 100g (3½oz) black treacle
- 2 tsp dried yeast
- 450g (1lb) plain flour, plus extra for dusting
- 1 tsp salt
- Vegetable oil, for greasing
- 1 large egg, lightly beaten, for glazing

Tip

Slashing the loaf allows it to continue rising in the oven, while the steam from the pan of boiling water gives the bread a good crust.

1 Heat the milk and 120ml (4fl oz) of water in a small saucepan. Bring to a boil and add the polenta. Cook for 1–2 minutes or until it thickens, then remove from the heat. Stir in the butter until well mixed. Beat in the treacle, then set aside to cool.

2 Dissolve the yeast in 100ml (3½fl oz) of warm water and stir well. Sift the flour and salt into a bowl and make a well. Gradually stir in the polenta mixture, then add the yeast mixture to make a soft, sticky dough.

3 Turn the dough onto a lightly floured work surface. Knead for about 10 minutes until soft and elastic. It will remain fairly sticky, but should not stick to your hands. Knead in a little flour if it seems too wet. Put the dough in a lightly oiled bowl, cover loosely with cling film, and let rise in a warm place for up to 2 hours. The dough will not double in size, but should be very soft and pliable when well-risen.

4 Turn the dough onto a lightly floured work surface and gently knock it back. Knead it briefly and shape it into a flattened oval, tucking the sides underneath the centre of the dough to get a tight, even shape. Place on a large baking tray and cover loosely with clingfilm and a clean kitchen towel. Let it rise in a warm place for about 2 hours. The dough is ready to bake when it is tight and well risen, and a finger gently poked into the dough leaves a dent that springs back quickly.

5 Preheat the oven to 180°C (350°F). Place one oven rack in the middle of the oven and another below it, close to the bottom. Boil a pot of water. Brush the loaf with a little beaten egg and slash the top two or three times with a sharp knife on a diagonal. Dust the top with flour, if desired, and place it on the middle rack. Place a roasting tin on the bottom rack, then quickly pour the boiling water into it and shut the door.

6 Bake for 45–50 minutes until the crust is nicely darkened and the bottom sounds hollow when tapped. Remove from the oven and allow to cool on a wire rack.

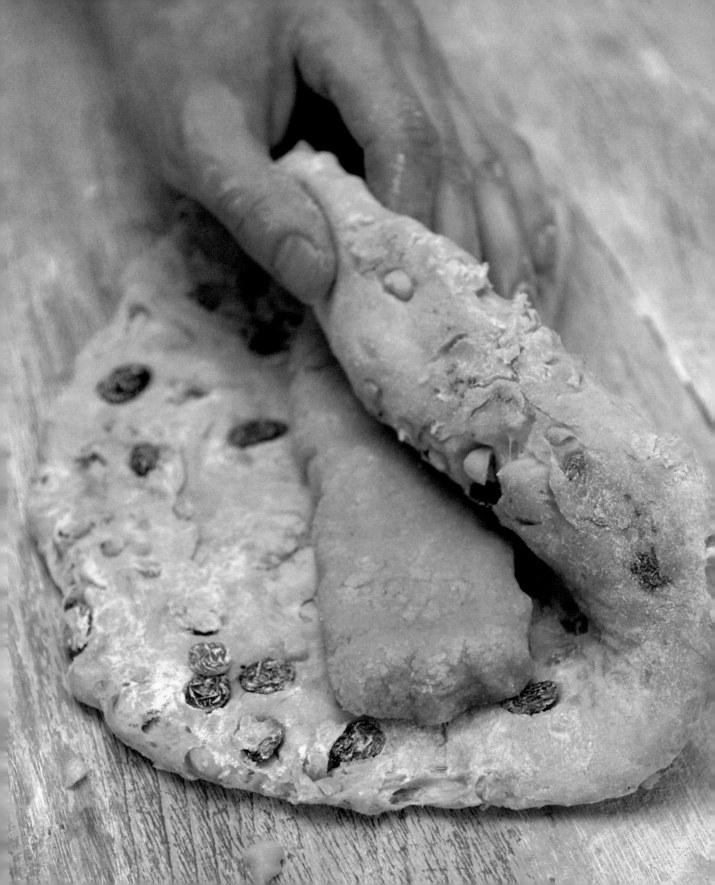

Stollen

This rich, German Christmas bread is filled with rum-soaked fruits and wrapped around an almond paste centre – symbolizing the baby Jesus wrapped in swaddling clothes. The loaf is baked if it sounds hollow when tapped on the base. As you let it cool on a wire rack, brush the top with melted butter, and then dust with icing sugar just before serving it.

1 Preheat the oven to 200°C (400°F). Put the dried fruit in a small bowl. Warm the rum in a pan and pour it over the fruit. Leave to one side to allow the fruit to soak up the alcohol.

2 Mix the flour, sugar, and spices, pour in the yeasty milk, and make a batter. Cover with a dry tea towel and leave in a warm place for half an hour. Then add the butter and egg.

3 Mix into a dough, knead for 8–10 minutes, and rest for 1–2 hours, or until doubled in size. Mix the filling ingredients into a paste. Knead all the fruits and nuts into the dough.

4 Roll the dough into an oval shape. Form the paste into a long roll, put it in the centre, fold the dough over the paste, brush the edges with milk, rest for an hour, and bake for 30 minutes.

Ingredients

- 75g (2½oz) sultanas
- 50g (1¾oz) currants
- 3 tbsp rum
- 375g (13oz) white flour
- 50g (1¾oz) caster sugar
- ½ tsp ground cardamom
- 1½ tsp ground cinnamon
- 2 tsp dried yeast mixed with 170ml (6fl oz) lukewarm milk
- 50g (1¾oz) butter, melted
- 1 egg, lightly beaten
- 50g (1¾oz) mixed peel, chopped
- 50g (1¾oz) almonds, chopped

For the almond filling
- 115g (4oz) finely ground almonds
- 50g (1¾oz) caster sugar
- 50g (1¾oz) icing sugar
- 1½ tsp lemon juice
- ½ egg, lightly beaten

Mini panettone

This sweet Italian Christmas bread is rich in butter, eggs, and dried fruits, yet it is deliciously light and soft. Italians traditionally have a slice of panettone with a glass of Champagne on Christmas day. Avoid leaving any dried fruit on the surface of the dough as you put it into the moulds, or it will burn in the oven and turn hard and bitter.

Ingredients

Makes 12 mini loaves

- 500g (18oz) unbleached white bread flour
- ½ tsp salt
- 1 tsp dried yeast
- 120ml (4fl oz) lukewarm milk
- 2 eggs
- 2 egg yolks
- 150g (5oz) butter, softened
- 75g (3oz) plus 2 tbsp caster sugar
- 115g (4oz) mixed peel, chopped
- 75g (3oz) raisins
- Melted butter for brushing

Equipment

- 12 mini pudding moulds

1 Preheat the oven to 180°C (350°F). Sift the flour and salt into a bowl. Make a well. Whisk the yeast, milk, and eggs together and pour into the well. Partially mix with the flour to make a batter.

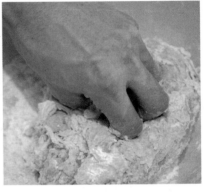

2 Rest the batter for 30 minutes. Add the yolks, butter, and sugar, and mix them and the rest of the flour into the batter with a fork. Bind the ingredients into a ball with your hands.

3 Knead the dough for 5 minutes and leave to rest in a warm, but not too warm, place for 1½–2 hours, or until doubled in size. Then scatter over the peel and raisins.

4 Gently knead in the peel and the raisins. Divide into 12, place in the moulds, cover with a dry tea towel, and rest for 1 hour. Then brush the tops with melted butter and bake for 20 minutes.

Stained-glass biscuits

The melted sweets in these biscuits look like tiny stained-glass windows when they catch the light. Make a mixture of some plain biscuits and some with sweet centres, and if you want to hang them from your tree as edible decorations, make a small hole in the top of each shape before baking them. The sweet mix is very hot as the biscuits come out of the oven, so take care.

Ingredients

Makes 12 biscuits

- 100g (4oz) butter
- 275g (10oz) caster sugar
- ½ tsp vanilla extract
- 2 eggs
- 525g (18oz) plain flour
- 2 tsp baking powder
- 2 tsp ground cinnamon
- ½ tsp salt
- A little milk
- A handful of organic hard-boiled sweets, crushed (put candies of one colour in a clean, recycled plastic bag and crush them with a rolling pin)

1 Preheat the oven to 190°C (375°F). Grease and line two large baking trays. Cream together the butter and sugar in a large bowl. Add the vanilla extract and stir in the eggs.

2 Sift the flour, baking powder, cinnamon, and salt into a separate bowl. Add the egg mix and then the milk, a little at a time, and mix into a dough. Chill for 30 minutes.

3 Roll out the dough on a lightly floured surface until 5mm (¼in) thick. Cut shapes using a cutter. Use a smaller cutter to make the holes, and fill each with a few crushed sweets.

4 Bake for 10 minutes. Leave the baked cookies on the paper and transfer the paper onto a wire rack. Allow the cookies to cool completely before removing them from the paper.

Chocolate brownies

Once packaged in an airtight tin, these irresistable chocolate brownies will stay their best for up to six days. Don't overcook them or they will lose their soft, fudgy quality; look for a dull crust to form, then quickly take them out of the oven. You can make the brownies in advance, freeze them, and leave them to thaw in a tin – there will be no excess moisture.

1 Preheat the oven to 190°C (375°F). Grease and line a 30 x 23cm (12 x 9in) baking tray with baking parchment. Put chocolate pieces and butter cubes in a bowl.

2 Melt the chocolate and butter slowly in a bain-marie: rest the bowl over a pan of gently simmering water on a low heat.

3 Dissolve the coffee granules in the water in a large bowl. Beat in the eggs, sugar, and vanilla extract. Then beat in the chocolate mixture.

4 Fold in the flour and chocolate chips. Pour the mix into the tray. Bake for 20–25 minutes, or until firm to the touch. Cut into squares once cool.

Ingredients

- 350g (12oz) plain chocolate, broken into small pieces
- 225g (8oz) butter, cut into small cubes
- 2 tsp instant coffee granules
- 2 tbsp hot water
- 4 eggs
- 225g (8oz) caster sugar
- 1 tsp vanilla extract
- 75g (3oz) self-raising flour
- 225g (8oz) plain chocolate chips or small chunks of plain chocolate

Shortbread

Shortbread is traditionally baked in ceramic moulds, or in a round tin and cut into petticoat tails or wedges, but use whatever shaped tray you have to hand for these crisp, yet wonderfully crumbly, biscuits. To make festive shortbread shapes, roll the dough out to a thickness of 3–5mm (⅛–¼in), cut the shapes with biscuit cutters, and bake in the oven for 12–15 minutes.

1 Preheat the oven to 150°C (300°F). Grease and flour a baking tray. Cream together butter and sugar in a bowl until the mix is pale. Sift and mix in flour and semolina, a little at a time.

2 Draw the mixture together with your fingertips to form a dough and tip it out onto a clean, lightly floured surface. Knead the dough to a smooth, uniform consistency.

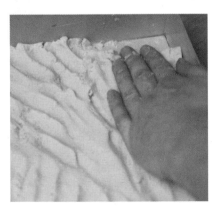

3 Put the dough into the prepared tray, press it down evenly, and prick it all over with a fork. Sprinkle sugar over the top and chill in the fridge for 15 minutes until firm.

4 Bake for 30 minutes or until pale brown in colour. Leave in the tray for 5 minutes, then slice into fingers, or triangles if you have used round trays, and leave to cool on a wire rack.

Ingredients

Makes 12 biscuits

- 225g (8oz) butter
- 100g (3½oz) caster sugar, plus extra for topping
- 275g (10oz) plain flour
- 50g (1¾oz) semolina

Tip

Kneading and freezing
Work quickly and lightly as you knead the shortbread dough: the butter in the mix will soften and turn greasy if you overwork the dough, so the less you handle it, the better it will taste when baked. The baked biscuits can be frozen for up to one month.

Marshmallow sweets

It's essential that you use a sugar thermometer to achieve the correct boiling point when heating the sugar solution in this recipe. The syrup is extremely dangerous at this high temperature, so take care and keep children well away from the pan. The marshmallows keep well for three to four days if stored in an airtight tin lined with baking parchment.

Ingredients

- 2 tbsp icing sugar
- 2 tbsp cornflour
- 25g (1oz) gelatine powder
- 125ml (4fl oz) hot water
- 2–3 drops food colouring (optional)
- 500g (1lb 1½oz) granulated sugar
- 250ml (9fl oz) cold water
- 2 egg whites

Tip

Toasting marshmallows

If children want to toast their marshmallows over an open fire, tie a fork handle securely to one end of a bamboo stick with a piece of string. Push a square of marshmallow onto the prongs of the fork and give the other end of the bamboo stick to the child to hold.

1 Lightly oil a cake tin. Mix the icing sugar and cornflour, sift a little onto the tin, then set aside. Dissolve the gelatine in the hot water in a small bowl. Add the food colouring.

2 Put the sugar and cold water in a large pan, stand a thermometer in the pan, and heat the sugar syrup to 122°C (252°F). In the meantime, whisk the egg whites until stiff.

3 Take the boiling syrup off the heat and mix in the dissolved gelatine. Then gradually beat the syrup into the beaten egg whites. The texture should be thick and creamy.

4 Pour the mix into the tin and leave to set in a cool place. Once cool, cut into squares. Lightly coat each square in the icing sugar and cornflour mix. Store in an airtight tin.

Chocolate brittle

A tower of chocolate brittle makes an impressive end to a good meal. This recipe is so simple that you can quickly make up extra quantities if you have supplies in the store cupboard. For the best-tasting brittle, buy milk and dark chocolate with a high cocoa content, and toast the nuts first in a heavy-based pan over a low heat, shaking them frequently until they are lightly browned.

1 Make each type of chocolate brittle separately. Break the chocolate slabs into small pieces and place them in a small bowl.

2 Melt the chocolate slowly in a bain marie (see p.197). Stir gently with a spoon every so often to make sure all the chocolate pieces melt.

3 Lift the bowl of melted chocolate from the saucepan of water and mix in the dry ingredients. Line a cake tin or baking tray with some cling film or baking parchment.

4 Pour the mix into the tray. Allow to cool. Refrigerate until solid. Just before serving, turn out onto a board, remove the parchment, and break into chunks with the tip of a knife.

Ingredients

For the white chocolate brittle

- 300g (11oz) organic white chocolate
- 150g (5½oz) macadamia nuts

For the milk chocolate brittle

- 300g (11oz) organic milk chocolate
- 100g (3½oz) hazelnuts
- 100g (3½oz) raisins

For the dark chocolate brittle

- 300g (11oz) organic plain chocolate
- 100g (3½oz) pecans
- 100g (3½oz) dried cranberries

Mince pies

Prepare the mincemeat ideally a week, or at the very least one day, ahead of making the pies to allow the flavours to develop. If the rolled pastry is too thick it won't cook quickly enough and the mincemeat will soak into it, turning it soggy; the right thickness results in a delicate, crispy pastry. These quantities should make 24 pies that will keep well for up to seven days in an airtight tin.

Ingredients

For the mincemeat

- 85g (3oz) each sultanas, raisins, and currants
- 35g (1½oz) blanched almonds, finely chopped
- ½ Bramley apple, cored and coarsely grated
- 100g (3½oz) dark muscavado sugar
- 50g (1¼oz) candied peel, chopped
- 75g (2½oz) dried cranberries
- Grated zest of 1 orange
- Grated zest of 1 lemon
- 1 tsp mixed spice
- 40g (1½oz) shredded suet
- 50ml (2fl oz) brandy

For the pastry

- 225g (8oz) plain flour
- 125g (4½oz) unsalted butter, diced
- A large pinch of salt
- 1 large egg yolk
- 1–2 tbsp hot water
- 2 tbsp milk
- 1 tbsp caster sugar

1 Mix the mincemeat ingredients in a bowl, put in a sterilized jar, and store in the fridge. For the pastry, mix flour, butter, and salt in a bowl. Add the egg and water. Form a dough.

2 Turn the dough onto a lightly floured surface and knead until smooth. Chill for 10 minutes in the fridge, then roll it out to 2mm (1/16in) thick and cut 24 discs with a cutter.

3 Preheat the oven to 190°C (375°F). Press each disc gently into the individual bases of a bun or pie tray. Fill each pastry case with a teaspoon of the mincemeat.

4 Top the pies with pretty shapes cut from the remaining pastry dough. Brush each with a little milk, sprinkle with caster sugar, and bake for 18–20 minutes or until golden.

Chocolate log

Known as a Bûche de Noel in France, this chocolate cake can be served as a dessert or with coffee. Bake the sponge in advance if you need to prepare ahead; to keep it moist, wet some greaseproof paper, wring it out, wrap it around the cooled sponge, and put the cake in a plastic bag. This will keep it fresh for a day or so until you are ready to roll and decorate it.

Ingredients

For the sponge

- 4 extra-large eggs at room temperature
- 100g (3¹/₂oz) caster sugar
- 65g (2¹/₂oz) self-raising flour
- 40g (1¹/₂oz) cocoa powder

For the filling

- 225g (8oz) can unsweetened chestnut purée
- 1 tbsp coffee essence
- 50g (1³/₄oz) caster sugar
- 150ml (5fl oz) plus 2 tbsp double cream, stiffly whipped
- 2 tbsp brandy

For the fudge topping

- 25g (1oz) melted butter
- 3 tbsp cocoa powder
- About 3 tbsp milk
- 225g (8oz) icing sugar, sifted

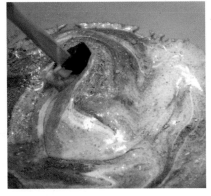

1 Preheat the oven to 200°C (400°F). Grease and line a Swiss roll pan. Whisk together the eggs and sugar until light, then sift in the flour and cocoa and fold into the mixture.

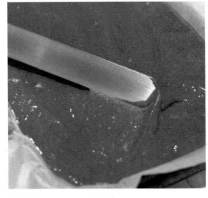

2 Turn the mix into the prepared pan and spread it evenly. Bake in a preheated oven for 10 minutes. Turn the cake out onto greaseproof paper and leave to cool.

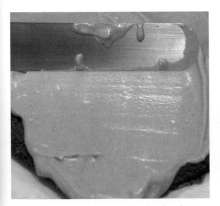

3 To make the filling, put the purée in a bowl and beat in the coffee essence and sugar until smooth. Fold in the cream and brandy. Spread the filling over the cooled sponge.

4 Peel off the paper as you roll the sponge up. For the topping, mix the butter and cocoa, add the milk and icing sugar, and beat until smooth. Decorate the cake to look like a log.

Plum pudding

Early November is an ideal time to make a plum pudding, as its flavour matures and improves with age. Plum puddings are traditionally set alight before being served: heat a saucepan, add two tablespoons of brandy, immediately light the brandy with a match, pour it over the pudding, and serve.

1 Sift the flour and spices into a large bowl. Add all the remaining dry ingredients and the apple and carrot, and mix well.

2 Mix the eggs into the mixture, one at a time, then add the orange juice and rind and stir well.

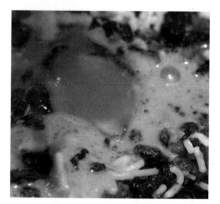

3 Add the stout, ale, or milk and mix thoroughly. Cut three circles of greaseproof paper that will fit inside the rims of the pudding basins, then butter the insides of the basins.

4 Decant the mix into the basins, packing it down. Cover with the paper and kitchen foil, and secure with string tied into a handle. Steam for eight hours, or in four two-hour stages.

Ingredients

Makes three 1¼ litre (3lb) puddings

- 175g (6oz) self-raising flour
- 1 tsp grated nutmeg
- 1½ tsp mixed spice
- 1 tsp ground cinnamon
- 90g (3oz) fresh white breadcrumbs
- 280g (10oz) beef suet
- 110g (4oz) dark brown sugar
- 450g (1lb) currants
- 900g (2lb) raisins
- 450g (1lb) sultanas
- 110g (4oz) candied peel
- 110g (4oz) flaked almonds
- 1 large cooking apple, grated
- 1 carrot, grated
- 6 eggs
- Juice and zest of 1 orange
- 600ml (1 pint) stout, ale, or milk

Equipment

- Three pudding basins
- Greaseproof paper
- Kitchen foil
- Length of string

Sachertorte

This classic Viennese dark chocolate cake is one of the world's most renowned grown-up cakes. It's quite dense and rich, and not overly sweet, so ideally it should be served in small slices with a little unsweetened whipped cream on the side, accompanied by a cup of coffee or tea. The Sachertorte will improve in flavour if you make it a day or so before you want to eat it.

Ingredients

- 150g (5oz) unsalted butter, softened
- 150g (5oz) plain chocolate, broken into pieces
- 100g (4oz) caster sugar
- ½ tsp vanilla extract
- 5 large eggs, separated, with the whites put into a large bowl
- 75g (3oz) ground almonds
- 40g (1½oz) plain flour

For the topping

- 4 tbsp apricot jam, melted
- 200g (7fl oz) double cream, mixed with 150g (5oz) plain chocolate, melted

1 Preheat the oven to 180°C (350°F/ Gas 4). Grease and line a round cake tin. Beat the butter in a large bowl or mixer until very soft. Meanwhile, melt the chocolate in a bain marie (p.197).

2 Add the sugar to the butter and beat until the mixture is light and fluffy. Add the vanilla extract and mix well. In a separate bowl, whisk the egg whites until stiff.

3 Add the melted chocolate to the mix, then the egg yolks, one at a time, followed by the ground almonds and flour. Add about one third of the egg whites and stir well.

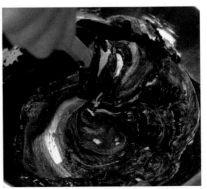

4 Fold in the remaining egg whites, pour into the tin, and bake for 35 minutes. Once cool, brush the jam over the torte, spread the chocolate and cream mix on top, and chill.

Gingerbread house

With its intricate piping and fondant cutout detail, this impressive gingerbread house is sure to please a crowd. If you do not wish to eat your beautiful finished creation, make sure to prepare and decorate additional gingerbread biscuits cut into festive shapes, such as trees or stars.

Ingredients

- 500g (1lb 2oz) royal icing, piping consistency (see p.218)
- Baked gingerbread house pieces (see pp.214–15)
- 100g (3½oz) red fondant, strengthened
- Cornflour, for dusting

Equipment

- Round-tipped piping nozzles (such as PME no. 1, 2, and 3)
- Piping bag
- 28cm (11in) white fondant-covered square cake board
- Craft glue
- 1m (3ft) red satin ribbon 1cm (½in) wide
- Square, heart and circle cookie cutters

1 Attach a no. 2 tip to a piping bag and fill it with white royal icing. Pipe tiles onto each roof panel in a series of loops. Change to a no. 1 tip, and pipe patterns and picot dots on the walls and the front of the house. Outline the windows and door, and pipe dots on the top of the chimney. Allow each piece to dry thoroughly; this can take up to 24 hours.

2 Assemble the baked gingerbread pieces into a house (see pp.214–15). Once dry and firm, carefully lift the house and dot the underside of the walls with royal icing. Place it onto a cake board covered with white fondant. Use craft glue to attach the ribbon around the sides of the board.

3 Put the chimney together, then attach it to the house. Use the spare panel to cut a 1cm- (½in-) wide strip, as long as the roof, to run along the top. Glue it to the roof top with royal icing.

4 Roll out the red fondant on a cornflour-dusted surface and use cutters for tiny hearts, circles, and a wreath for the door. Roll small balls with your hands. Allow to dry overnight.

5 Once all the pieces are dry, use a no. 1 tip to pipe royal icing onto the wreath in dots. Switch to a no. 3 tip, and decorate the joins of the house with piped beading, then pipe a snail train around the base of the house.

6 Glue the fondant shapes to the house with royal icing and allow it to harden thoroughly.

Gingerbread recipe

The secret to a successful gingerbread construction is good-quality dough, a symmetrically drawn template, and precise baking time. You will also need patience, as you must wait for the glue or royal icing fixative to dry as you construct, to ensure a sturdy finished product.

Ingredients

- 175ml (6fl oz) golden syrup
- 115g (4oz) butter, softened
- 115g (4oz) brown sugar
- 600g (1lb 5oz) plain flour, sifted, plus extra for dusting
- 4 tsp ground ginger
- 1 tsp ground cinnamon
- 4 tsp bicarbonate of soda, dissolved in 4 tsp cold water
- 2 large egg yolks

Equipment

- Rolling pin
- Cardboard or baking parchment templates (see p.248)
- Palette knife

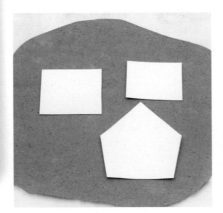

1 Preheat the oven to 180°C (350°F). Melt the syrup, butter, and sugar in a pan. In a bowl, sift together the flour, ginger, and cinnamon, and make a well.

2 Stir in the bicarbonate of soda mixture, egg yolks, and melted syrup mixture. Knead into a pliable dough on a flour-dusted surface.

3 While the dough is still warm, roll it out to about 5mm (¼in) thick. Lay out the templates, then use a sharp knife to neatly cut around them.

4 Transfer the pieces, including a spare panel, onto a lined baking tray. Bake for 10–13 minutes, or until firm and just beginning to brown.

Homemade Edible Treats

Building with gingerbread

When building your gingerbread house, make sure to assemble the pieces on or beside the board on which it will be presented. Handle your house with care, and only once completely dry, to minimise the possibility of pieces shifting.

1 If the pieces have any rough edges or have spread in the oven, trim them back into shape with a sharp, hot knife. Leave the pieces to cool.

2 Once cool, pipe your designs on the gingerbread pieces in royal icing (see p.212). Leave to dry fully.

3 Assemble your creation. First, build the walls by applying royal icing or sugar glue (see Tip) to the joins with a palette knife.

4 Once dry, attach the roof with icing or glue, holding it in place until it sets. Finally, assemble the chimney pieces and affix to the roof.

Ingredients

- Baked gingerbread house pieces (see opposite)
- Royal icing, piping consistency (see Royal icing, p.218)

Equipment

- Sharp knife
- Cake board

Tip

To make sugar "glue", melt 250g (9oz) white granulated sugar in a heavy-based pan over medium heat, until the sugar melts and browns. Be careful, since it can burn. Spread onto the gingerbread edges to glue pieces together. It will be very hot, so handle with care.

Festive fruitcake

This simple yet elegant Christmas cake is covered in smooth royal icing and topped with a delicate robin run-out. Piped icicles decorate the top and a pretty fondant bow encircles the fruitcake, which can be made weeks in advance of your special celebration.

Ingredients

- Icing sugar, for dusting
- 1 batch marzipan (see p.220)
- 25cm (10in) fruitcake (see p.219)
- 90ml (3fl oz) apricot glaze
- White vegetable fat, for greasing
- 150g (5½oz) piping-consistency royal icing (see p.218)
- 750g (1lb 10oz) royal icing (see p.218)
- Red, brown, yellow, and black colouring pastes
- Edible pearl lustre dust
- Cornflour, for dusting
- 200g (7oz) red fondant, strengthened

Equipment

- Fondant roller
- Robin templates (see p.239)
- Masking tape
- Food-grade acetate sheets
- Piping bags with fine piping tips (such as PME no. 1 and 2)
- Turntable or lazy Susan
- Offset palette knife
- 30cm (12in) round cake board, iced with royal icing
- Multi-ribbon cutter, straight sides
- 1m (3ft) white satin ribbon (1cm/½in wide)
- Craft glue

1 Four days before you want to serve the cake, roll out the marzipan to 5mm (¼in) thick on an icing-sugar dusted surface. Brush the surface of the cake with apricot glaze, and cover with marzipan. Set aside to dry for 2–3 days.

2 While the marzipan is drying, prepare the robin run-out. Trace the template on a sheet of paper. Use masking tape to secure it to a flat surface. Cover with acetate and secure with masking tape. Lightly grease the surface with vegetable fat.

3 Place half of the piping-consistency royal icing in a bowl, double-wrap with cling film, and set aside. Divide the remainder into four small pots. Using toothpicks, stir through colouring paste to achieve the different colours needed for the robin. Add just a dot of colouring paste at a time – a little goes a long way.

4 Fit a small tip (no. 1) to each piping bag, and fill each with a different colour. Using the right colour for each part of the robin (e.g. yellow for the beak), pipe the outline of each part of the robin. Make sure that all the lines touch each other. Keep the piping bags upright with a wet sponge around the tip, to prevent them from drying out. Make a second outline for the robin's wing on a separate sheet of acetate. Allow to dry for a few hours. Decant each piping bag into its own bowl and cover tightly with cling film. Set aside.

5 When the outlines are hard, thin the coloured icings, one by one, with some water, adding a drop at a time until it reaches the right consistency. Transfer each icing batch to a piping bag fitted with a slightly bigger tip (no. 2), and begin your run-outs (see p.221). Allow each section to dry for about 10 minutes before moving on to another colour. Fill in the second robin's wing in the same way. To achieve a good shine, allow to dry in a warm, dry place for several days.

continued overleaf

continued from previous page

Royal icing

Makes 750g (1lb 10oz)
- 3 large free-range pasteurized egg whites
- 700g (1¾lb) icing sugar, sifted, plus extra if needed
- 1 tsp lemon juice
- 2 tsp glycerine

Whisk the egg whites in a large bowl until foamy. Add the icing sugar a spoonful at a time. Stir in the lemon juice and glycerine and beat until stiff, thick, and peaks begin to form. Thicken with extra icing sugar as necessary.

Piping-consistency royal icing
Follow the steps given above, omitting the glycerine, and adding extra icing sugar until the mixture reaches the consistency of toothpaste.

While this recipe is very similar to traditional royal icing, the omission of glycerine makes it more appropriate for detailed piping work and gingerbread houses, when it needs to dry hard.

6 When the marzipan on the cake has dried, place the cake on a turntable. Apply a layer of royal icing to the marzipan with the palette knife, covering the sides first. Allow to dry, then apply another coat. Dry and add another layer of icing until the sides are smooth. When the sides are dry, ice the top, following the same steps. Try to get a sharp edge where the sides meet the top. Allow to dry.

7 Place the cake on the royal-iced cake board, taking care to centre it. Attach a no. 1 tip to one piping bag and a no. 2 tip to the other. Fill the bags with the remaining piping-consistency royal icing. Pipe a row of dots onto the surface of the cake, where the top meets the sides. Create icicles by piping dots that become a little smaller as you work down the cake in vertical lines. Make the lines uneven in length, to provide a more realistic effect. When dry, dust the dots with pearl lustre dust.

8 Dust a flat surface with cornflour, and roll out the red fondant to 2mm (¹⁄₁₆in) thick. Use the multi-ribbon cutter to cut a ribbon long enough to wrap around the base of the cake, 2cm (¾in) wide. Moisten the back and wrap around the cake with the seam at the front. Roll out another length of red fondant and create a bow. Moisten the back and apply to the cake at the seam.

9 Very carefully lift the dry robin run-out from the acetate sheet, using a thin metal palette knife. You may have to move the knife gently from side to side to release it. Affix to the centre of the cake with a small dot of royal icing. Dot a little royal icing onto the robin's wing portion of the run-out, and then carefully lift the wing on top, guiding it into place with your fingers. Allow to dry for about an hour.

10 Glue the satin ribbon around the base of the iced cake board, using craft glue. Pipe a few icicle dots over the seam at the back of the cake.

Fruitcake recipe

This rich, dense cake is a Christmas staple. Prepare it weeks in advance, store it in several layers of baking parchment in an airtight tin, and gradually feed the cake with brandy, a spoonful at a time. This will ensure it has a great flavour by the time you are ready to decorate and serve it.

1 Simmer the first seven ingredients in a large pot for 20 mins, until most liquid is absorbed. Remove from the heat. Allow to soak overnight.

2 Preheat the oven to 160°C (325°F). Beat the butter and sugar until fluffy. Mix in the eggs, one at a time.

3 Gently fold in the fruit mix and almonds. Sift over the rest of the dry ingredients and fold in, keeping the batter light and fluffy.

4 Pour into the tin and cover with foil. Bake for 2 hours. Uncover and bake for half an hour, or until a skewer comes out clean. Allow to cool in the pan for 10 minutes, then turn onto a cooling rack.

Ingredients

- 200g (7oz) sultanas
- 200g (7oz) raisins
- 350g (12oz) prunes, chopped
- 350g (12oz) glacé cherries
- 2 small desserts apples, peeled, cored, and diced
- 600ml (1 pint) sweet cider
- 4 tsp mixed spice
- 200g (7oz) unsalted butter, softened
- 175g (6oz) dark brown sugar
- 3 large eggs, lightly beaten
- 150g (5½oz) ground almonds
- 275g (9½oz) plain flour
- 2 tsp baking powder
- brandy, for soaking (optional)

Equipment

- 25cm (10in) deep, round cake tin, greased and lined

Marzipan

Marzipan is a thick, sweet almond paste that is traditionally used to cover fruitcakes underneath royal icing or fondant. It can also be coloured and shaped by hand to create 3D cake decorations. Its high sugar content allows it to last for months without refrigeration.

Ingredients

Makes 900g (2lb)

- 175g (6oz) caster sugar
- 300g (10oz) icing sugar, sifted, plus extra for rolling and kneading
- 450g (1lb) ground almonds
- 1 tsp pure vanilla extract
- ½ tsp orange juice
- 2 large eggs, beaten

Equipment

- Palette knife

Tip

Marzipan has a soft texture and will dry hard. If you wish to create marzipan decorations, make sure to keep them in an airtight container once dry.

1 Mix both the sugars and ground almonds in a bowl. Make a well in the centre and add the vanilla extract, orange juice, and eggs.

2 Use a palette knife to fold the wet ingredients gently into the dry ingredients, until you have a crumbly dough.

3 Dust a flat surface with icing sugar, and knead the marzipan until smooth. Add more icing sugar, if needed, to get the right consistency.

Royal icing run-outs

Using royal icing (see p.218 for recipe), you can create a variety of delicate run-out designs, from simple white snowmen to multi-coloured robins. To create a unique run-out design for your cake, draw your own festive image to use as a template.

1 Divide and colour the royal icing as required. Lay an acetate sheet over your template, so that the design is visible. Lightly grease the acetate with vegetable fat.

2 Fill a fine-tipped piping bag with royal icing. Pipe outlines around the shape, including internal lines for any different-coloured areas. Allow to dry for a few hours to create a dam.

3 Water down the remaining royal icing until it reaches flooding consistency (see Tip). Divide and colour as required. Attach the large nozzle to a piping bag, and fill with icing. Flood each area, working from the centre outwards until it is fully covered. Repeat for all colours and spaces.

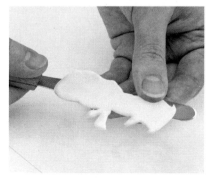

4 Gently tap the board or surface beneath the shape to release any air bubbles. Allow to dry for 24 hours. Lift the decoration away from the acetate sheet with a palette knife and carefully apply to the cake with a dab of royal icing.

Ingredients

- White vegetable fat, for greasing
- Royal icing
- Colouring paste (optional)

Equipment

- Food-grade acetate sheets
- Templates (see p.239)
- Piping bags
- A small, fine, circular piping tip and a large circular piping tip
- Palette knife

Tip

To make flooding-consistency royal icing, carefully add water to piping-consistency royal icing drop by drop until it is roughly the consistency of shampoo. Draw a spoon through the surface. If the line created fills in 10 seconds, it is ready.

Prepare Christmas drinks

Winter is the time to enjoy warming drinks to keep the chilly weather at bay, so if you want to serve something other than Champagne or wine, try these fruity seasonal drinks. The Old-fashioned rum with a twist takes a little more time and care to prepare than the others, but it's worth the effort.

Old-fashioned rum with a twist

Put the honey and 1 tablespoon of rum in a Rocks glass. Stir the mixture until the honey has mixed into the rum. Add 1 ice cube and 1 mint leaf and stir until the ice has nearly melted. Add another tablespoon of rum and another ice cube. Stir until the ice cube has partly melted. Add the rest of the rum and one more ice cube. Stir the drink 15 times or so and then fill the glass to the top with ice cubes. Take a piece of pared lime rind, crack it over the glass to release the oils from the skin, and serve.

Ingredients

For each drink:
- 25ml (1fl oz) honey or golden syrup
- 50ml (2fl oz) aged rum
- Ice cubes
- 1 fresh mint leaf
- Pared lime rind, to garnish

Spiced fruit cocktail

Peel and slice the pear and place it in the bottom of a cocktail shaker. Add the plum jam and ground cinnamon and muddle down (a muddler is a barman's wooden utensil used to crush hard ingredients to release flavours; the handle of a wooden spoon can be used instead). Add the Cognac, apple juice, and some ice. Shake and strain the mixture into a cocktail glass, add a few drops of lemon juice, and serve.

For each drink:
- 1 pear
- 1 tsp plum jam
- 1 pinch ground cinnamon
- 50ml (2fl oz) Cognac
- 50ml (2fl oz) apple juice
- Ice cubes
- A few drops of fresh lemon juice

Fruit fizz

Put some ice cubes into a tall tumbler or highball glass. Pour in equal amounts of the orange juice, cranberry juice, and lemonade. Stir well and serve.

For each drink:
- Ice cubes
- ⅓ glass fresh orange juice, chilled
- ⅓ glass cranberry juice, chilled
- ⅓ glass organic lemonade, chilled

Make flavoured alcohol

If you gather blackberries from hedgerows in the autumn, or if you have a bountiful harvest of raspberries or other fruits, turn some of the crop into fruity flavoured alcoholic drinks. Use gin or vodka with the highest proof content to get the best preserving results. These wonderfully warming drinks take three and a half months to mature, and then continue to improve in flavour.

Alcohol is a preservative – nothing can grow in pure alcohol – and when fruits are soaked in it, the alcohol absorbs their flavour to give a fruity taste and colour. Use ripe produce for the best quality and flavour and freeze the fruits until needed. Frozen fruit provides excellent results: the freezing process ruptures the fruit skins and allows the juices to flow out.

To make Raspberry gin

Ingredients

To make about 1 litre (1¾ pints):

- 700ml (1¼ pints) bottle of gin
- 400g (14oz) raspberries, fresh or frozen
- 250g (9oz) caster sugar
- A few cloves (optional)
- 1 stick of cinnamon (optional)
- A few drops of almond essence (optional)
- 1 large, wide-necked jar, sterilized, or 2 empty gin bottles

Pour the gin, fruit, sugar, spices, and almond essence into the sterilized jar, or divide the ingredients equally between two bottles using a funnel (there's no need to sterilize a vodka or gin bottle if the alcohol has just been poured out of it). Seal and store in a cool, dark place. Give the jar or bottles a shake daily for the first two weeks and then weekly for a further three months. During this time the sugar dissolves and the liquid takes on a luscious red colour. Take a sip every now and then and add more sugar if needed. After three and a half months, or when the taste is to your liking, strain the ingredients, and re-bottle the liquid only.

Variation To make Sloe gin, replace the raspberries with sloes and prick each sloe berry with a skewer before adding to the gin. To make Blackberry or Damson vodka, replace the gin with vodka and the raspberries with blackberries or damsons.

Use a muslin bag to strain the alcohol and fruits. Suspend the muslin using two bamboo sticks and collect the alcohol in a bowl.

Make mulled drinks

Winter is the time to enjoy warming drinks to keep the chilly weather at bay. Mulled drinks have long been part of our winter traditions: mead – a fermented drink made of honey, water, and yeast – was flavoured with spices and sometimes fruits, and heated by plunging a hot poker into the liquid; and wassail, a hot, spiced punch often associated with winter celebrations in northern Europe, derives from medieval times, when it was more like a mulled beer seasoned with spices and honey. These drinks are easy to prepare and taste delicious.

Mulled wine can be left warming on the hob all evening, but don't let it boil or the alcohol will evaporate. If you want to prepare it ahead of time, heat the wine, spices, lemon peel, sugar, and the orange studded with cloves to simmering point, turn off the heat, and leave to marinate for a few hours before adding the orange juice, brandy, and orange slices.

Mulled wine

Pour 2 bottles of red wine into a large pan and add 1 orange studded with 12 cloves, the pared rind of 1 lemon, a 5cm (2in) piece of fresh ginger, peeled and cut into slices, 2 cinnamon sticks, 4 tablespoons of brandy, 125g (4½oz) demerara sugar, the juice of 1 orange, and 1 thinly sliced orange. Bring almost to the boil on a medium heat, stirring until the sugar has dissolved. Turn the heat down and simmer for 30 minutes, then serve in glasses.

Hot pear cup

Cut half an apple into slices and stud each slice with a couple of cloves. Place the slices in a large pan, add 1 litre (1¾ pints) pear cider, 1 vanilla pod, 1 large piece of pared lemon zest, 150ml (5fl oz) brandy, 1 cinnamon stick, 2 tablespoons of honey, and bring to the boil. Simmer gently for 10 minutes, then serve in four glasses.

Winter whisky sour

Stud 4 lemon slices with 3 cloves each. Place in a pan with 1 strip of lemon rind, 2 tablespoons of maple syrup, and 400ml (14fl oz) water. Bring to the boil, then turn off the heat. Leave to infuse for 5 minutes. Divide 100ml (4fl oz) whisky and the 4 lemon slices between four glasses, discard the lemon rind, add the infused water, and serve.

Mulled-wine kit

For family and friends who enjoy mulled drinks over Christmas (see pp.226–27), a mulled-wine kit is the perfect gift. When you tie the spice sachet to the bottle, add a gift label with instructions for making the mulled wine and what other ingredients to add (see below). One kit should be enough for about six glasses.

1 Prepare the spices: break the cinnamon stick into three pieces, crush the cardamom pods lightly, and grate a little fresh nutmeg.

2 Place the cinnamon, cardamom, nutmeg, and cloves in the centre of the muslin square. Measure out the ginger and add it to the spices.

3 Gather the four corners of the muslin and hold them with the fingertips of one hand. Gather up the four remaining corners.

4 Wrap the piece of twine around the top of the sachet and secure it tightly. Then tie the loose ends of the twine around the neck of the bottle.

Ingredients

- 1 cinnamon stick
- 6 cardamom pods, lightly crushed
- Fresh nutmeg
- 12 cloves
- 1 pinch ground ginger
- 1 bottle red wine

Equipment

- 1 square muslin, about 18 x 18cm (7 x 7in)
- A length of twine

Mulled wine instructions

Put the wine, sachet, 150ml (¼ pint) of water, and 6 tbsp granulated or demerara sugar into a pan. Heat gently until the sugar has dissolved, but do not boil. Ingredients to add: a splash of brandy, gin, Cointreau, port, or the juice of 1 orange.

Templates

Fabric garland

See pages 16–19. Make templates of the shapes that you like and cut out two of each shape, except for the robin's body and beak, for which you should cut out one of each shape, and the holly leaf, for which you should cut out four shapes.

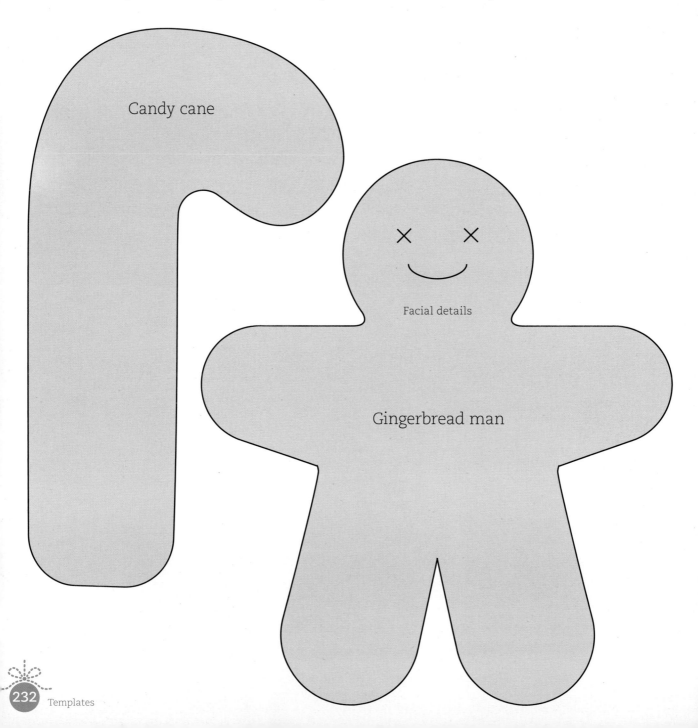

Candy cane

Facial details

Gingerbread man

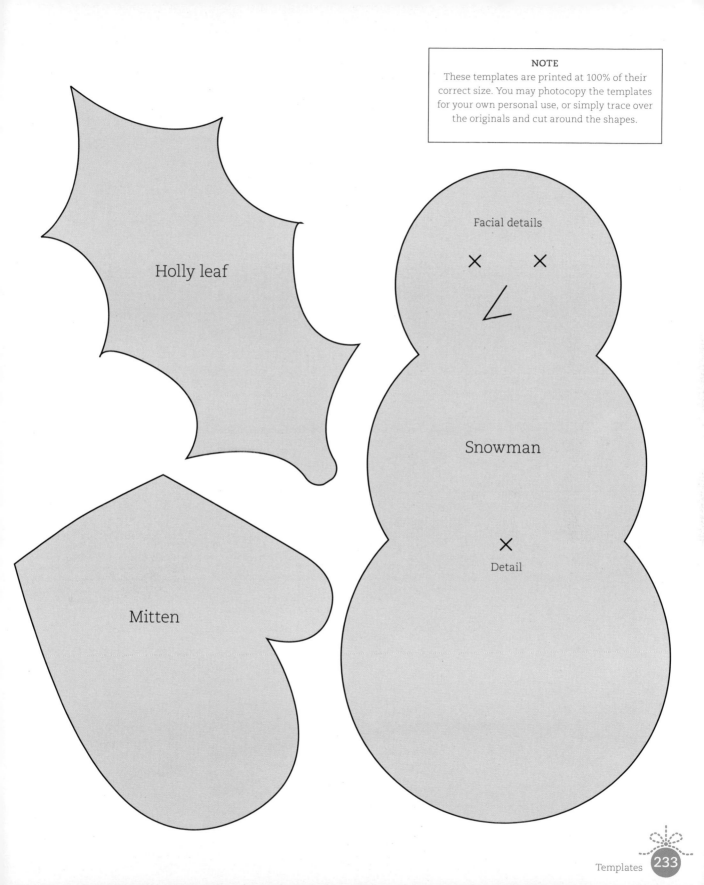

Holly leaf

Facial details

Snowman

Detail

Mitten

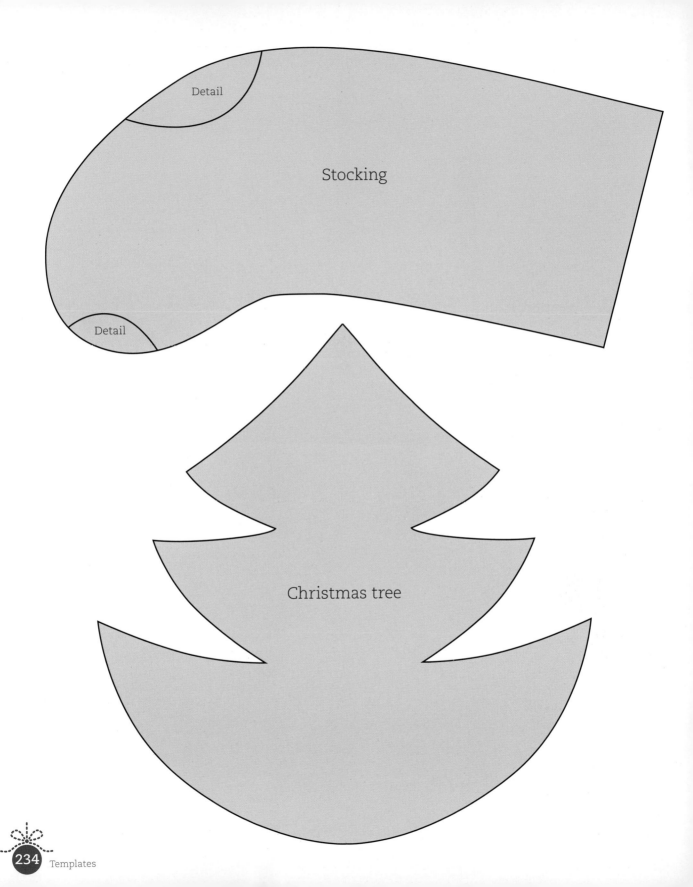

Stocking

Detail

Detail

Christmas tree

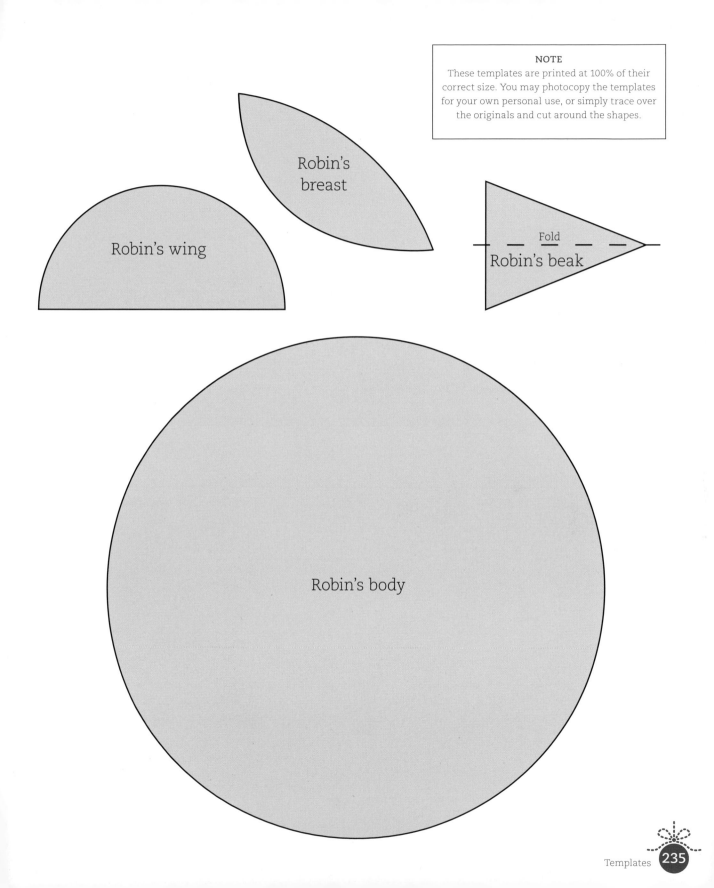

Scented fabric hearts

See pages 56–57. For each fabric heart, cut two shapes from the template.

Seam line

NOTE
These templates are printed at 100% of their correct size. You may photocopy the templates for your own personal use, or simply trace over the originals and cut around the shapes.

Peg doll tree angel

See pages 60–61. Make up the templates and cut out two angel dress shapes in fabric and one wing shape in felt.

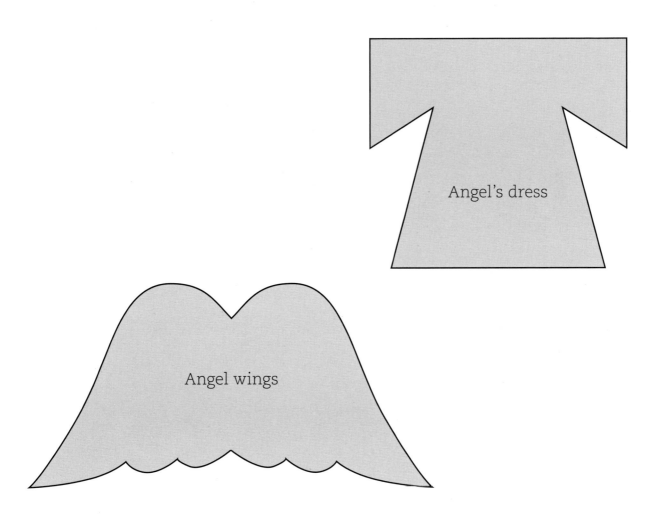

Angel's dress

Angel wings

NOTE
This template is printed at 50% of its correct size. You may photocopy the template for your own personal use. Scale up 200% on a photocopier.

Festive birds

See pages 50–51. For each bird, make up the templates and cut out two body shapes, two wing shapes, and several flowers and leaves.

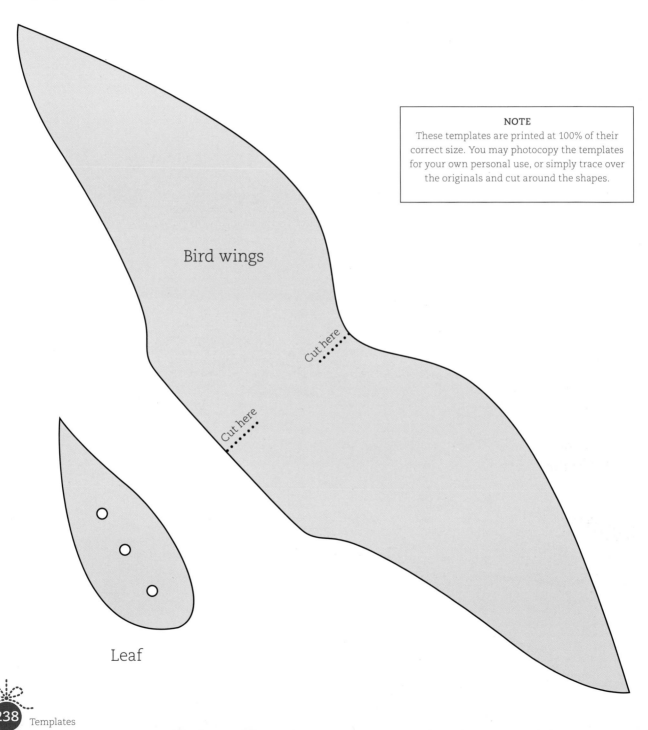

Bird wings

NOTE
These templates are printed at 100% of their correct size. You may photocopy the templates for your own personal use, or simply trace over the originals and cut around the shapes.

Cut here

Cut here

Leaf

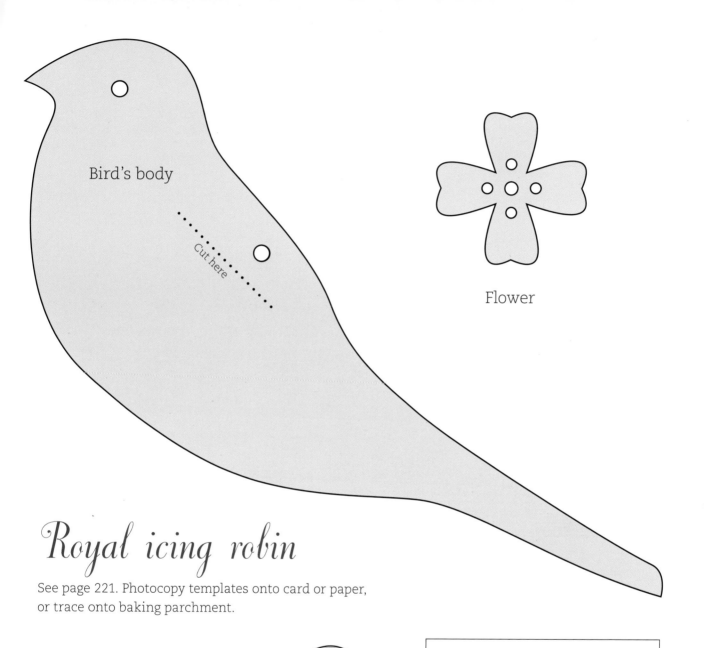

Bird's body

Cut here

Flower

Royal icing robin

See page 221. Photocopy templates onto card or paper, or trace onto baking parchment.

Wing

Run-out robin

NOTE
This template is printed at 50% of its correct size. You may photocopy the template for your own personal use. Scale up 200% on a photocopier.

Paper and fabric cards and decorations

See pages 54–55, 136–37, and 140–41.

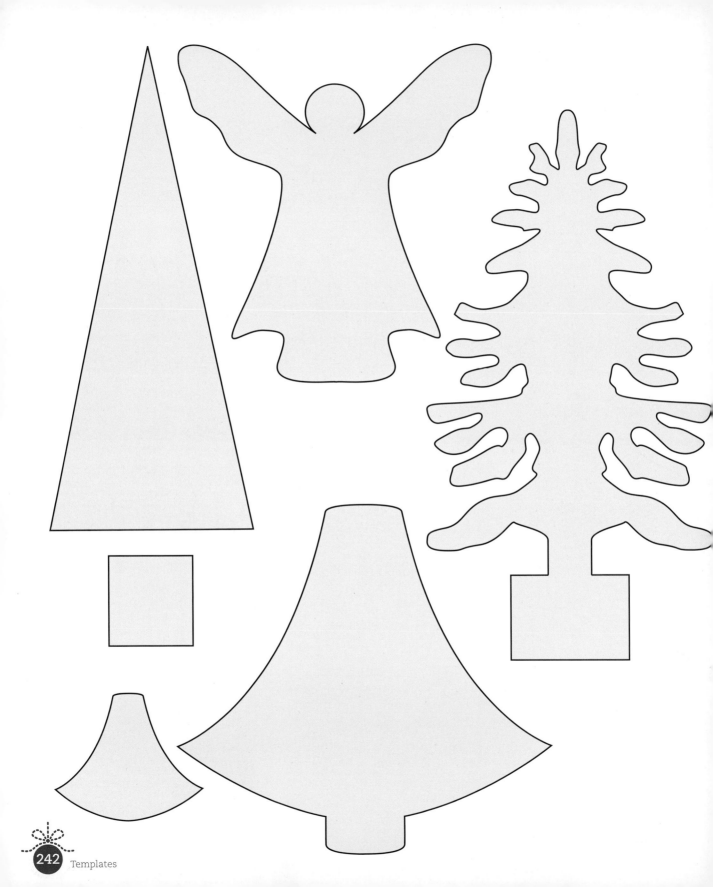

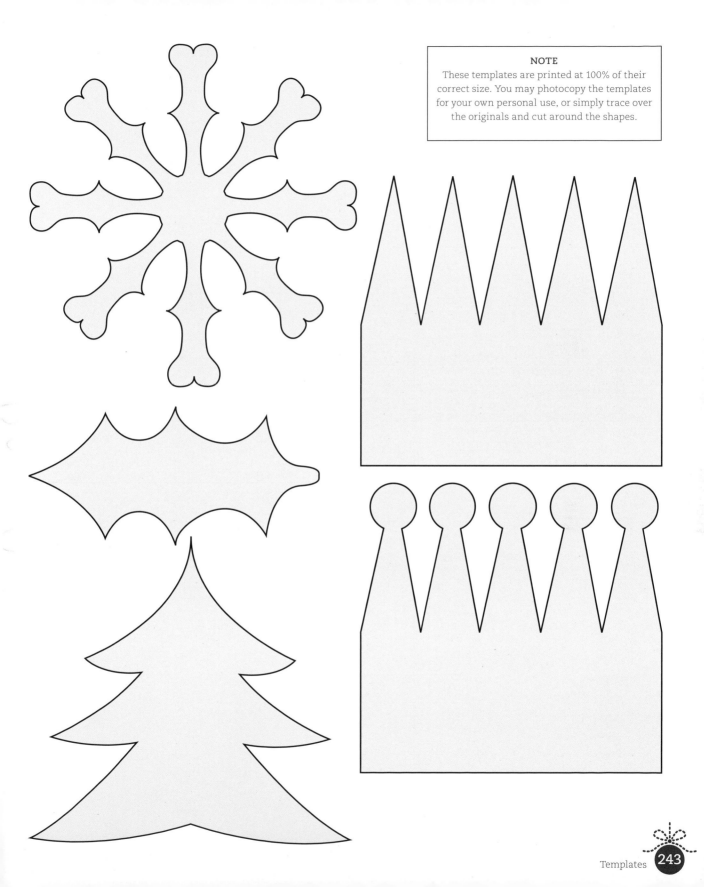

Advent calendar sacks

See pages 58–59. For each sack, cut out two shapes from the template.

Seam line

Silver clay jewellery

See pages 104–109.

**Leaf
template**

**Heart keyring
template**

**Button
cufflink
templates**

**Wallpaper
earrings
template**

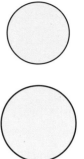

NOTE
These templates are printed at 100% of their
correct size. You may photocopy the templates
for your own personal use, or simply trace over
the originals and cut around the shapes.

Hot-water bottle cover

See pages 126–27. For each hot-water bottle cover, cut out one shape from the front
cover template, and one shape from each of the back cover templates. Cut out two
shapes from either the heart or star template.

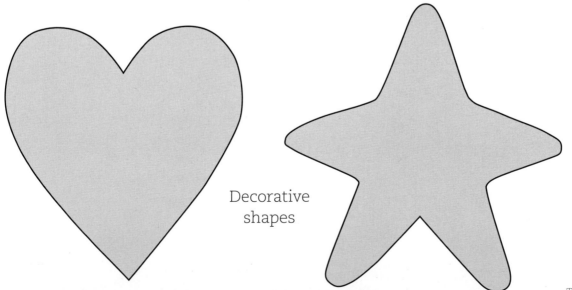

**Decorative
shapes**

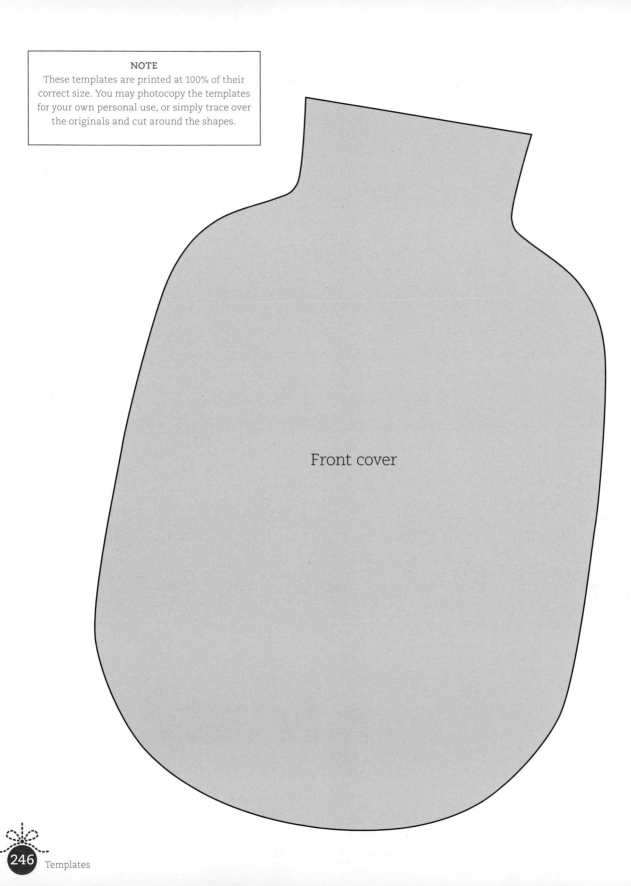

Front cover

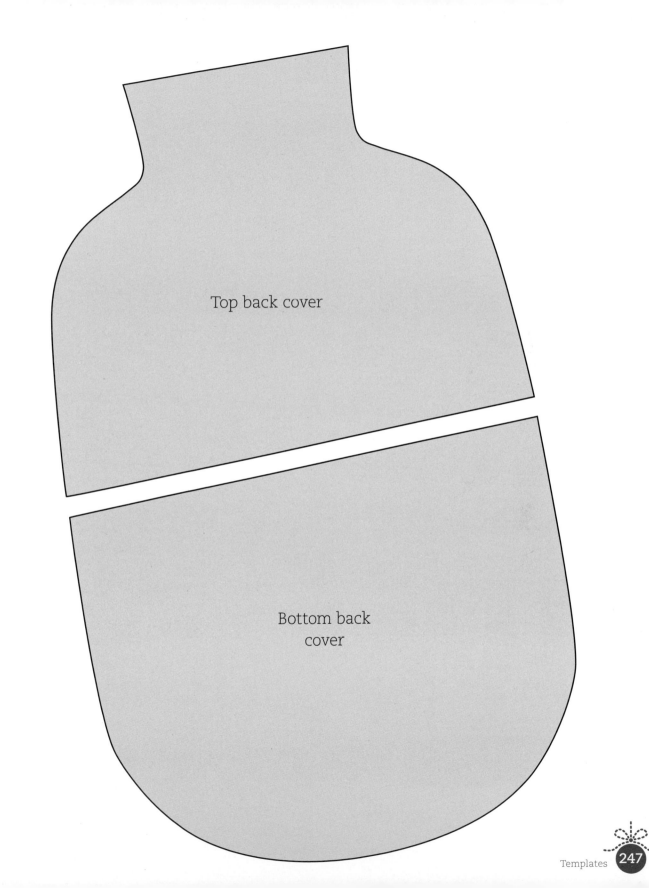

Top back cover

Bottom back cover

Gingerbread house

Scan and use these panels to cut out gingerbread pieces to build your Gingerbread house (see p.212–5).

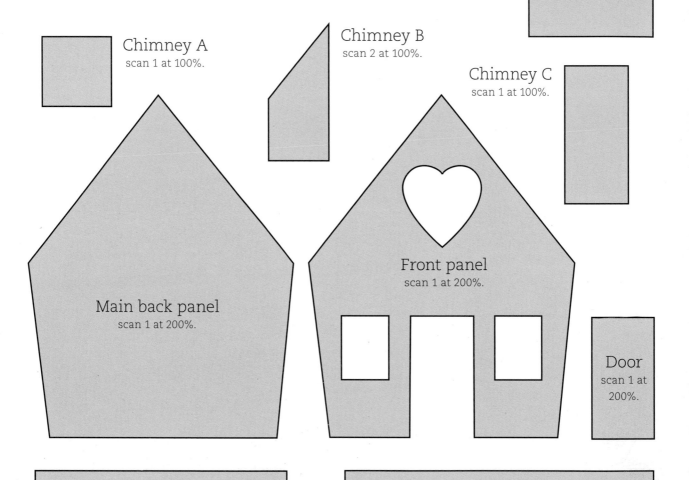

Chimney A
scan 1 at 100%.

Chimney B
scan 2 at 100%.

Chimney C
scan 1 at 100%.

Chimney D
scan 1 at 100%.

Main back panel
scan 1 at 200%.

Front panel
scan 1 at 200%.

Door
scan 1 at 200%.

Wall panels
scan 2 at 200%.

Roof panel
scan 2 at 200%.

Square gift box template

This template makes the box on pp.148–49.
Please enlarge to the required
size on a photocopier.

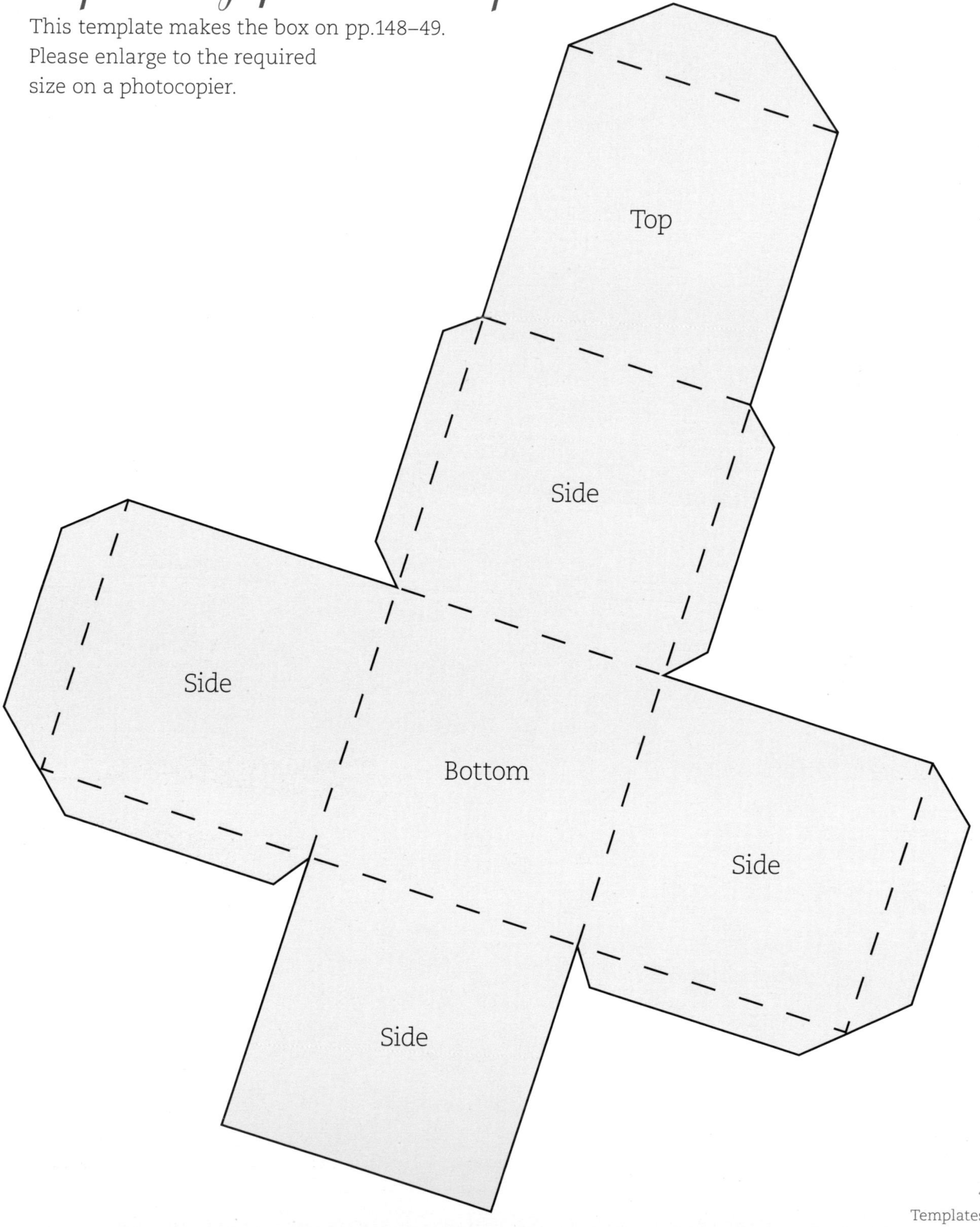

Top

Side

Side

Bottom

Side

Side

Jewellery case template

This template makes the box on pp.142–44.
Please enlarge to the required size on a photocopier.

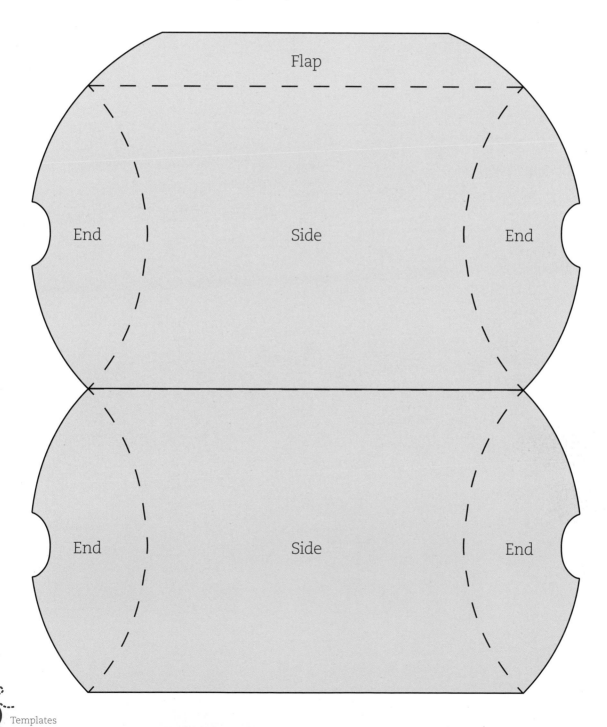

Flap

End Side End

End Side End

Pyramid box template

This template makes the box on pp.146–47.
Please enlarge to the required size on a photocopier

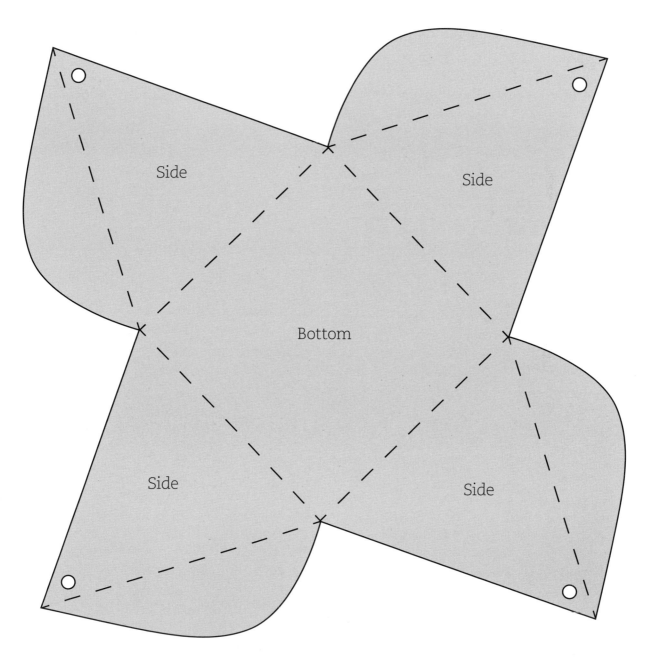

Side

Side

Bottom

Side

Side

Index

Penguin Random House

Editorial Assistant Amy Slack
Design Assistant Philippa Nash
Producer, Pre-Production Tony Phipps
Senior Producer Ché Creasey
Creative Technical Support Sonia Charbonnier
Managing Editor Stephanie Farrow
Managing Art Editor Christine Keilty

First published in Great Britain in 2016 by
Dorling Kindersley Limited
80 Strand, London WC2R 0RL

Material previously published in:
The Christmas Book (2008),
Flower Arranging (2011), Craft (2012),
Canapés (2012), Family Kitchen Cookbook (2013),
Handmade Gifts (2013), and
Step-by-Step Cake Decorating (2013)

Copyright © 2008, 2011, 2012, 2013, 2015, 2016
Dorling Kindersley Limited
A Penguin Random House Company
10 9 8 7 6 5 4 3 2 1
001–300889–Oct/16

A CIP catalogue record for this book is available
from the British Library

ISBN 978-0-2412-7533-7

Printed and bound in China

All images © Dorling Kindersley Limited
For further information see: www.dkimages.com

A WORLD OF IDEAS
SEE ALL THERE IS TO KNOW

www.dk.com

Acknowledgments

Sheherazade Goldsmith would like to thank: Susannah Steel for writing the book and agreeing with all my ideas and edits. Jo Fairley for her workable beauty recipes. Ted and Harry for the prettiest recycled fabric decorations I have ever seen, and all the crafts people; Barbara Coupe, Francine Raymond, Lucy Harrington, Made in Hastings, Sparrowkids, Isabel de Cordova, and Caroline Zoob. Richard Scott for his delicious recipes and Kirsty Trotter for her endless patience. Peter Anderson for his beautiful photographs and everyone at DK. Lastly, my kids for making Christmas so much fun.

DK would like to thank: US Consultants Meg Leder, Kate Ramos; US Editors Shannon Beatty, Christy Lusiak, Margaret Parrish, Rebecca Warren; Project Editors Hilary Mandleberg, Corinne Masciocchi, Laura Nickoll, Scarlett O'Hara, Laura Palosuo, Susannah Steele; Project Art Editors Charis Bhagianathan, Jane Ewart, Gemma Fletcher, Glenda Fisher, Sara Robin, John Round, Ivy Roy, Caroline de Souza; Photographers Peter Anderson, Clive Bozzard-Hill, Ruth Jenkinson, William Reavell; Crafters Barbara Coupe, Lucy Harrington, Charlotte Johnson, Made in Hastings, Claire Montgomerie, The Oxford Soap Company, Francine Raymond, Clare Smith, Sparrowkids, Ted & Harry; *Cake Decorating* author Karen Sullivan; Cake Decorator Sandra Monger; Fiona Corbridge, Valerie Lane-Glover and Pammie Riggs for valuable advice; Mike Wells; Jane at Not Just Food Ltd and Kate Blinman for testing the recipes; Angela Baynham for proofreading; and Vanessa Bird for the index. For their work on the previous edition of this title, DK would also like to thank Vanessa Hamilton, Elizabeth Yeates, Vanessa Hamilton, Rebecca Fallowfield, and Alison Donovan.